Aussie land

Aussie Yarns

Kel Richards

STRAND PUBLISHING
Sydney

Aussie Yarns
Copyright © 2004 Kel Richards

First published 2005 by Strand Publishing

ISBN 1876825413

Distributed in Australia by:
Family Reading Publications
B100 Ring Road
Ballarat Victoria 3352
Phone: 03 5334 3244
Fax: 03 5334 3299
Email: info@familyreading.com.au

Edited by Owen Salter
Cover design by Joy Lankshear
Typeset by Midland Typesetters, Maryborough, Victoria
Printed by McPherson's Printing Group, Maryborough, Victoria

Contents

G'Day!

Collected together in this book are a bunch of yarns I've been spinning for a while. Some are puzzle stories (with a challenge to you to solve them!); some are parables; some are fables; and some are bush ballads. Towards the end there's even a tribute to one of my heroes—Dr Paul White (the great Jungle Doctor).

They've been pulled together to give you pleasure—and I hope they do. So gather round the campfire, put the billy on to boil and enjoy the yarns.

Kel Richards

The Puzzle of the Stolen Streeton

Rain was falling steadily in the little outback town of Yallambee. Drought had gripped the district for many months, and quite a few local farmers and graziers had been struggling to survive. Now the rain had started and hope was in the air.

The town's one and only policeman, Constable Clancy Paterson, and his young wife Matilda (otherwise known as Matty), knew that Tom Mosley was one of those closest to being driven off his property—by the length of the drought that had just broken, and by his string of accumulated debts. So they were delighted when he had a piece of good news: he'd inherited a valuable painting from an elderly aunt who had lived in Sydney.

When the painting arrived at Tom's sheep station on the outskirts of Yallambee, it was reported—and photographed—in the district newspaper, *The Wongalla Daily Leader*.

Matty Paterson fetched *The Australian Encyclopaedia* from the shelf while Clancy poured himself a second cup of tea.

'Here it is,' she said, leafing through the pages, 'the entry on Sir Arthur Streeton.'

'So this painting Tom Mosley has inherited,' said her husband, 'is definitely a Streeton then?'

'So the paper said.'

'Well, read out what you've got there about Streeton, then, sweetheart.'

Matty turned a page and said, 'Well, he lived from 1867 to 1943. He was one of the Australian impressionists, and his most famous paintings are held by the National Gallery of Victoria and the Art Gallery of New South Wales. It says here, "His work gave respectability to the Australian landscape as a legitimate art subject." And according to the *Leader*, the painting Tom has inherited was painted in the mid-1890s, during Streeton's Blue Mountain period. I'd really like to see it, honey.'

As she added those last words she looked winningly at her husband.

'Well, then,' said Clancy, 'why don't I give Tom a call and ask him if he minds if we drop in to see him later in the day?'

'Wonderful,' said Matty.

Clancy made the phone call, and Tom Mosley invited him and Matty to call in for afternoon tea that same day. Clancy did his morning patrol of the town and spent the rest of the morning doing the paperwork he hated.

Then, after lunch, he and Matty drove in the police patrol van out of town, off the bitumen, and onto the gravel road that led out to Tom's sheep station. After they turned off the road onto the property Matty hopped out at each fence to open and close each gate as they drove through.

When they reached the home yard they saw the front door of the homestead standing open—even the fly screen—and the place deserted.

They parked the van and ran through the light rain up onto the verandah.

'Tom!' called out Clancy. 'Are you there, Tom? It's me and Matty.'

There was no reply, but as both the front door and the screen door were standing open they walked in.

'He shouldn't leave the screen door open like this,' said Matty. Then she added, 'And Clancy, you'd better wipe your boots or you'll traipse mud all over Tom's clean floor. There's not a mark on it, so don't you go and dirty it up.'

Just then Tom staggered out of the lounge room holding a handkerchief to his forehead.

'What's happened, mate?' asked Clancy.

'Been robbed,' grunted Mosley.

'Let's have a look at that forehead of yours,' said Matty, prising up the handkerchief. Underneath were a cut and a bruise.

'It doesn't look too bad,' she said. 'I'll get some Dettol and a bandage and clean it up for you. Where's your first aid kit?'

Clancy made Tom sit down in an armchair and got him to tell his story.

'Well, it's that painting by Sir Arthur Streeton that's been stolen. The big oil painting that I inherited from Aunt Rose.'

'Yes, we read about it in the paper,' said Clancy.

'Well,' explained Tom, 'I was standing in front of the painting—that's where it hung, right there, on that wall opposite, in that big empty space . . . it was quite a big painting. Anyway, I was standing in front of it, looking at it, admiring it, like . . . I'd just finished fixing up the insurance for it, you see. Then there was a noise, and reflected in the glass covering the painting I saw someone running in off the verandah behind me. But before I could turn around he hit me. I dropped unconscious, and when I woke up the painting was gone.'

'Oh, that's terrible!' said Matty as she re-entered the room, carrying a bowl of warm water and the first aid kit.

'Can you describe this man?' said Clancy.

'Sure, I got a good look at him, as I say, in the reflection of the glass covering the painting. He'd be about my height, with red hair and a thick drooping moustache. He was wearing a blue shirt. Well, what about it Clancy— do you think you cops can catch him and get my painting back? Or will I have to claim on the insurance?'

Constable Clancy Paterson stood up with a disgusted look on his face. 'We can't recover something that hasn't been stolen, Tom. The story you've just told me is a load of old rope. And there are four clues proving that your story is untrue.'

What are those four clues? (Solution at the end of the next yarn.)

Check the Map!

Don and Emily were driving down a country road in their four-wheel-drive. They'd bought the vehicle twelve months earlier, and as they'd used it to drive around the suburbs they'd heard all the jokes from their friends and neighbours about it being a four-wheel-drive that never saw the dirt.

They'd heard their friends laughingly call their top-of-the-line vehicle a *Balmain bulldozer*, a *Bronte buggy*, a *Double Bay* or *Mosman* or *Rose Bay shopping trolley*, a *North Shore tank* or a *North Shore Kingswood*. After hearing all these jokey names countless times Don and Emily decided they would take their next holiday in the bush—off the bitumen, where only a four-wheel-drive could go.

And that's what they were doing.

Before leaving Birdsville they'd reported to the local police station and lodged their travel plans. They carried plenty of water and all the provisions more experienced travellers had told them to pack.

But the problem was—the map. The dirt roads seemed at times to blend into the red dust of the outback, and signposts were *very* few and *very* far between. So Don and Emily were dependent on the map they carried.

Don drove as Emily read the map. But after a while Emily began to worry.

'Are you sure we're on the right road, Don?' she asked as she gnawed her lower lip.

'You're the one with the map,' replied her husband. 'Are *you* sure?'

'But what if the map's wrong?' continued Emily. 'What if the map's out of date or something like that? If we get lost out here we'll be in dreadful trouble.'

There was a note of rising panic in her voice, so Don said quietly and patiently, 'In the first place, are you certain you're reading the map correctly, and you've got us on the road the map says we should be on?'

'Oh, yes,' said Emily with confidence. 'I've got no doubt about that. I'm really following what the map says. I've checked and double checked and triple checked, so I'm quite certain of that.'

'So,' continued Don patiently, 'it all boils down to whether the map is reliable or not, doesn't it?'

'Yes . . . I guess that's what I'm worried about.'

'Well then, Emily my love, turn over the map and look at the back. What does it say?'

'Ah, let me see . . . there's this year's date.'

'That's good, isn't it? That means the map's up-to-date. What else do you see printed on the back of the map?'

'It says here: "Based on a new survey by Australian Army engineers." '

'So then,' continued her husband. 'It boils down to this: do you trust the Australian Army engineers to get their mapping right?'

Emily thought for a moment before replying, 'Yes, I do.'

'Then,' said Don, 'you can relax—we're following a reliable map, and being well and properly guided.'

Moral: Life's journey depends on having reliable guidance.

The map, the guidebook, God has provided to guide us through our life's journey is the Bible: 'All Scripture is breathed out by God and profitable for teaching, for reproof, for correction, and for training in righteousness' (2 Timothy 3:16).

'All Scripture' means the whole of the Bible, and 'breathed out by God' means 'directly inspired by God'. This book, the Bible, has been put together under God's guidance and direction and contains just what God wants it to contain—nothing more and nothing less.

Its four functions are to give us (1) teaching, (2) reproof, (3) correction and (4) training in righteousness. Those four functions hit all the points of the compass. That is a complete list of what we need on the journey of life.

Solution to 'The Puzzle of the Stolen Streeton'

Clancy explained the four clues as follows:

1. Tom claimed to have seen his attacker's reflection in the glass covering the painting, but everyone knows that oil paintings are not framed under glass—so that can't be true.
2. Even if there had been a glass over the painting, he could never have seen as much detail as he provided in his description in just a fleeting glance—it was an impossible amount of detail.
3. He claimed he had been hit from behind, but his wound (self-inflicted, of course) was on his forehead.
4. There were no marks on the floor—it was spotless—but if a thief had run in from outside (where it had been raining) and across the floor there would have been muddy footprints or marks.

The moral from this mystery: Life leaves its marks.

One of those four clues was the absence of marks on the floor. If someone in muddy boots had crossed that floor there would have been marks. And in just that way, life leaves its marks.

Has your Christian faith left its marks on your life? If you were charged in a court of law with being a Christian, would there be enough evidence to convict you? Jesus said that following him should leave its marks: 'By this all will know that you are My disciples, if you have love for one another' (John 13:35 NKJV).

What marks has your life left on you?

And what marks have you left on the lives of others around you?

The Ballad of the Two Sons

(Luke 15:11–32)

Near the town of Bundiwallop,
Where the sun sets in the west,
Was a sheep and cattle station
By the name of 'Come-and-Rest'.

Sam McPherson was the owner
(A top bloke—the best of men)
And Sam was Dad to two sons:
One was Dave, the other Ben.

Now Dave, he was the older,
Made for work and not for fun,
While Ben was lighter hearted,
He was Sammy's younger son.

One day when in the home yard
Sam and Ben were dipping sheep,
Ben asked his Dad a question
That knocked Sam in a heap.

'Dad, I know you'll die one day,
You'll tumble off the twig,
And I'll inherit half the property
And a chance to make it big.

'Well, Dad, you know the truth is
I'd rather have it now.
You see, I wanna leave the farm
And forget the sheep and cows.

'I wanna hit the big smoke, Dad,
With some dough I can invest.
Dad, I wanna get away from
This farm called "Come-and-Rest".'

'But, son, I thought you liked it here'
Was all his Dad could say,
'Cause Ben's request had sort of
Taken Sammy's breath away.

Reluctantly Old Sam said, 'Yes,
Let Ben his fortune seek',
And gave Ben all the paddocks
To the west of Snakebite Creek.

The stock and station agent
Came and did a deal with Ben,
Brought a contract for the paddocks,
Ben whipped out his fountain pen.

Ben packed his clothes into a port,
In his wallet put his dough,
Shook hands with Dave and hugged his Dad,
Then turned his back to go.

Ben ended up in Sydney,
Where he opened an account
In one of the better known banks,
With a fairly large amount.

But the money ran though Ben's young hands
Like water through a sieve,
He made some flash new city 'friends'
Who said: 'We'll show ya how to live.'

Eventually Ben found his way
To a place they call Kings Cross,
And being rather naive,
What he thought was gold, was dross.

Ben's brain just overheated,
He rioted and rambled,
He fell in with the wrong crowd
And drank and drugged and gambled.

His new friends gathered round him
Saying, 'Ben is great, we think.'
And that is what they all said . . .
When Ben was buying drinks!

Eventually the dough ran out
And every buck was spent,
And Ben just couldn't figure out
Just where the money went.

Wherever all that money went,
It had certainly shot through.
And when the money ran out,
Ben's 'friends' all did so too.

And at the very moment,
Just to make things more depressin',
The national economy
Collapsed in a recession.

So Ben began to hitch-hike,
With his swag his only load.
Ben went back to the bush again:
Looked for work upon the road.

Eventually he got a job
At a dingy little farm.
They hired Ben as pig-man,
A job without much charm.

They didn't pay or feed him much
As he sloshed about the sty.
Ben said, 'These pigs are eating
Much better food than I.'

'I'm working in this pig-yard
Where I slop and feed and dig—
Why, I'm just another animal,
Just a vertical pig!

'The stockmen on Dad's station,
Back home on "Come-and-Rest",
Are better off than I am;
Perhaps I should head west.

'I'll go back to my father.
I'll say: "Dad, I got it wrong,
I turned my back on you and God,
Turned my back for far too long."

'I'll say: "Dad, I know I've given up
The right to be your son,
So I'll come back as a farm hand,
If you can use an extra one".'

So he went. He passed through Bundiwallop,
Then he climbed the last steep hill,
And in the distance spied a figure,
Someone waiting for him—still.

Through the dust that always blows about
The western slopes and plains,
Ben saw a waiting figure
Beside that dusty, outback lane.

The figure ran towards him,
Ben saw it was—his Dad!
Old Sam he wept, and Ben wept too,
They wept from feeling glad.

Then Ben he said his piece:
'Dad, I know I got it wrong,
I turned my back on you and God,
Turned my back for far too long.'

But Sam gave Ben a great big hug;
He could barely speak for tears.
The only words that Sam said were:
'After all these years!'

Sam found his best Akubra
And put it on Ben's noggin,
And gave him brand new leather boots
(His own were worn out sloggin').

Sam took him back to the homestead,
To a farmhand said: 'Hey you!
Go and kill that poddy calf,
It's time for a barbecue!

'The one who was dead is now alive,
This is my boy, my Ben,
My son who was completely lost,
Has now been found again.'

Now the stockmen liked their boss, Old Sam,
And they shared the old man's joy.
And, truth to tell, they quite liked Ben,
And were pleased to see the boy.

So they killed the calf and butchered it
While the western breezes blew,
And they built a fire and gathered round
And began the barbecue.

One bloke was missing from the feast,
He was out on the edge of the run,
Mending the boundary fences.
That was Dave—Sam's elder son.

As Dave rode back to the homestead,
He could hear the laughter and song
Carried upon the dusty wind
And thought: 'Now what's going on?'

When Dave rode into the home yard
On his big black gelding horse
He was told, 'Your brother Ben's come back,
So we're having a barbie, of course.'

Dave went all quiet and sulky
And muttered, 'So that's what it is.'
He refused to go into the party
And worked himself into a tizz.

Sam came out to talk to Dave,
And Dave said, 'Dad, be fair,
I've slaved away like a navvy,
And sometimes I think you don't care.

'You never said to have my friends
Around for a barbecue.
You never offered to give me a feast
Of a scrawny chook or two!

'I'll bet my brother wasted his dough
And it ran right through his paws.
I reckon most of it ended up
In the hands of Kings Cross whores!'

Sam grabbed Dave and gave him a hug,
Saying, 'Son, you're always here,
And I do appreciate the fact
That you never cause trouble or tear.

'But the one who was dead is now alive,
Your brother is back, our Ben,
My son who was completely lost,
Has now been found again.'

The Puzzle of the Shooting Accident

The phone call from Bert Dawson sounded urgent. 'Clancy, mate, can you get here pretty quick?' came his voice down the line.

Constable Clancy Paterson hung up the phone, called out to his wife Matty that he was driving out to Jindawarabell sheep station, and hurried out to where the police patrol van was parked in the driveway of the Yallambee police cottage.

Leaving the town Clancy went off the bitumen and followed the dusty, bumpy road that wove between the gum trees. Finally he turned off to the sheep station that was his destination, rattled over a cattle grid and took the track up to the homestead.

He entered the house to find three men waiting for him. Two of them he knew—Bert Dawson and old Doc Moran, the town's GP—but the third man was a stranger.

The introduction was made by Bert.

'Glad you're here, Clancy,' grunted the old farmer. 'This is Tom Goldfinch. Come up from Sydney for a weekend's shooting. It was Tom who first alerted us to the fact that Fogarty was missing.'

Clancy asked who Fogarty was.

Bert replied that Frank Fogarty was another weekend guest—also up for the 'roo shooting—and that his body had just been found in an old hut down where Wattle Creek ran through the property.

Doc Moran piped up to say, 'According to what we've been told it might be that there are—as you blokes say—"no suspicious circumstances", if you take my drift.'

'You're suggesting,' responded Clancy, 'a case of suicide?'

The four of them piled into Bert's old ute and set off across the paddock. Speaking quietly so as not to be overheard by the others, Clancy asked Bert what he knew of these two men—Tom Goldfinch and Frank Fogarty.

'I made a bit of a mistake, old mate, inviting those two here on the same weekend—a bad blunder,' rumbled Bert. 'Seems they were enemies. Bad blood between 'em, so I'm told. I didn't know that, of course, otherwise I would have made sure they weren't here on the same weekend. I met 'em separately—down in Sydney—and invited 'em up for a spot of shooting. And both just happened to suggest the same weekend. Well, I didn't see a problem with that . . . at least, not until they arrived. From the moment they clapped eyes on each other the air was damned frosty. And just a moment ago Goldfinch told me the story.'

Dawson went on to explain that, as Tom Goldfinch had told him, the two men had once been business partners: Goldfinch and Fogarty, Wool Merchants. It appeared that Fogarty systematically cheated Goldfinch, embezzling a large sum of money from their joint venture. This, Dawson explained, was not just Goldfinch's account of events; it was what a subsequent court case determined. However, for complicated legal reasons Fogarty got away with it. And there'd been a deep and abiding hatred between the two men ever since.

'This bitterness has gone on for years,' said the farmer. 'Tell me, Clancy, why do some men never get over these things? Red-hot anger when someone cheats you I can understand. But to nurse that anger and feed it for years is beyond me. Why does it happen?'

'Dunno,' replied Clancy. 'Forgiveness is costly—that's for sure. Whoever forgives pays the cost of whatever it is that needs to be forgiven. These two appear not to have been willing to pay the cost of forgiveness. So Goldfinch nurtures and grows an ugly bitterness over being cheated, and Fogarty likewise—over what, in his case? Perhaps over the fact that Goldfinch took him to court? Pride, arrogance, self-importance—all those things get in the way of burying the hatchet and getting on with life.'

For a time they drove in silence—or as silent as it can ever be in a ute rattling over a paddock—both thinking about the slow burning anger of bitterness that grows inside a man like a tumour until it finally poisons his whole system.

They arrived at the old hut and Doc Moran led the way inside. The others stood around while Moran examined the corpse. Frank Fogarty was lying on his back, a gaping wound in his chest and his hands around a shotgun.

'Is there a suicide note?' asked Clancy. Careful searching revealed that there was not.

When the doctor straightened up, Bert Dawson said, 'What can you tell us, Doc?'

'Well,' replied the GP cautiously, 'there'll have to be a post-mortem examination, but I'm certain it was the gunshots that killed him. Both barrels of the shotgun have been discharged, and from the appearance of the wound in the chest it's fairly certain they were not discharged simultaneously, but one after the other. And they were discharged at very close range—you can see the burn marks where the barrels were pressed against his shirt. From the way his hands are wrapped around the barrel and the stock and trigger, he could certainly have done it himself.'

At this point Tom Goldfinch piped up to say, 'And I think he did . . . do it himself, that is.' Then he added, 'And I'm not surprised. They say suicide is the coward's way out, and Fogarty always was a coward. If he was feeling guilty he would never have come to me and said he was sorry—he would have done this.'

'The coroner will have to be notified,' said Doc Moran, 'and it'll be up to him whether he wants the detectives from Wongalla to investigate. But he may be satisfied with a report from you, Clancy.'

Clancy knelt down beside the corpse and examined it more closely.

Rising to his feet again he said, 'Just tell me again, Mr Goldfinch, what happened this afternoon.'

A little uncomfortably Goldfinch cleared his throat and retold the story that the others had heard before, although Clancy was hearing it for the first time. He said that after lunch Fogarty and he had set out across the paddock together, but not pleased with the idea of spending the afternoon in each other's company, they'd parted when they reached creek, agreeing to meet back at the old hut two hours later. Goldfinch said he kept this rendezvous but Fogarty failed to make an appearance. He didn't think to look inside the hut; he simply called Fogarty's name repeatedly for ten minutes and then returned to the homestead to report Fogarty's disappearance. Bert Dawson then sent some of his boys out searching, and the body was quickly found—in exactly the condition in which it lay before them.

All eyes turned to the policeman, who said grimly, 'There are four reasons why this was not, in my view, suicide. Is there anything further that you want to tell us, Mr Goldfinch?'

What are the four clues that suggest to Clancy that this death was murder, not suicide? (Solution at the end of the next yarn.)

Ginger and the Giant Dog

![barbed wire divider]

Somehow Ginger had managed to antagonise one of the dogs of the suburb. This was strange because Ginger got on well with dogs as a rule. But there was this one dog that had taken a dislike to him . . . and the dislike was mutual.

Ginger wasn't clear exactly what breed of dog it was. The only thing that was clear was that it was a very big dog. It belonged to old man Stevens, who lived in an ancient house behind the railway line. And old man Stevens was a bad tempered old chap who was notorious for hating small boys. The fact that he grew fruit trees in his backyard that small boys sometimes raided may have started this animosity, but it had spread way beyond fruit trees.

At the sight of a small boy approaching his property, or even looking as if he might approach his property, old man Stevens went completely bananas. He cursed and swore and threw any heavy object that lay close to hand. The same attitude to small boys had somehow rubbed off on his dog. And that was why this particular dog, this big dog, hated Ginger.

If Ginger was walking down the street the dog started to growl on the other side of the fence as soon as Ginger approached. And because the fence was in bad repair, the dog sometimes escaped. Then Ginger had to run for his life.

During the Boy Scouts 'Bob-a-Job' week, one of his mates dared young Ginger to go and knock on old man Stevens' door and ask him for a job. Ginger couldn't resist a dare so he said he would. He crept up the path, constantly watching for the savage dog. He knocked nervously on the front door. When it opened he began to explain that he was there on behalf of the Boy Scouts, but before half a dozen words had got out of his mouth old man Stevens had turned and shouted to the dog in the hallway behind him, 'Get him, Fang! Kill! Kill!'

The dog shot out of the dark hallway towards Ginger on the front steps. Ginger didn't wait but turned and took off at the speed of a moon rocket being launched. He shot through the front gate, leaving it open behind him, and kept on running.

That was how the dog got out. And it stayed out for almost a week. For the whole of that week Ginger was terrified of coming around the corner and finding old man Stevens' giant dog confronting him on the footpath.

And then it happened. Ginger was coming home from the paper shop, having run a message for his Dad, when he turned a corner and found the dog—in the middle of the footpath, confronting him, crouched as if about to spring, and growling a deep threatening growl that came from the back of its throat.

But then Ginger made an amazing discovery. He found that as long as he faced the dog it came no closer. If he tried to retreat it pursued him, but when he faced it, it froze in its tracks. And when he approached it threateningly it even retreated a few steps.

Moral: Dangers need to be faced and resisted.

'Your adversary the devil prowls around like a roaring lion . . . Resist him, firm in your faith . . .' (1 Peter 5:8–9).

The word 'adversary' translates a Greek word commonly used for an opponent in a lawsuit. So the devil is like one who would sue you, take all that you have, and perhaps have you thrown in prison.

The word 'devil' itself translates the Greek *diabolos*, the usual word used for the Hebrew name 'Satan'—which means 'slanderer' or 'accuser'. Satan, or the devil, is he who would attack Christians by taking their good name away from them by slanders and accusations.

And the devil is called a 'lion': the metaphor conveying the strength and destructiveness of the devil, and accentuating the need for alertness and resistance on the part of Christians.

Solution to 'The Puzzle of the Shooting Accident'

Clancy ticked the four reasons off on his fingers as he spoke:

1. There was no suicide note. That's very rare among people who commit suicide—they usually leave something.
2. There were two shots fired, not one. Most people who commit suicide with a gun make sure they use just one shot. If the shot fails they're usually found injured but alive—firing a second shot is almost unheard of.
3. The shots were fired through the clothing—that's extremely rare in cases of suicide. If you murder a man you shoot him where he stands, in the clothes he's wearing, but those who commit suicide almost always press the gun barrel up against their body.
4. Most remarkable of all, the gunshot wounds are to the chest. Suicides almost inevitably point the gun barrel at the head or mouth.

Then Clancy said, 'Any one of those on its own would make me wonder—all four of them together make me certain. I repeat: Mr Goldfinch, is there anything further you want to tell us?'

There was a long, heavy silence in that small room as three pairs of eyes fastened on Tom Goldfinch. But he wasn't looking at them; he was looking down at the corpse.

Finally he spoke in a whisper, more to himself than anyone else: 'And I'd do it again,' he said. 'I'd gladly do it again.'

The moral from this mystery: Forgiveness is costly.

Forgiveness is costly—as Clancy Paterson said. And whoever forgives pays the cost. The Bible says: 'God shows his love for us in that while we were still sinners, Christ died for us' (Romans 5:8).

The Day the Creek Broke Its Banks

(Matthew 7:24–27)

They were mates and they were neighbours—
Bluey Banks and Clancy Stone.
They'd often meet down at the pub,
Or natter on the phone.

Their stations were adjoining—
Two nicer farms you couldn't seek.
The dividing line between them was
A stream called 'Lambing Creek'.

Blue and Clancy and their families
Decided they would build
Themselves two brand new houses,
By the creek, not on the hills.

To the north of Lambing Creek,
Clancy's fancy slowly rose,
Upon a shelf of solid rock
Above the water where it flows.

But Bluey built his dream house
On a sloping, sandy flat,
Even closer to the water,
On a beach is where it sat.

And when their homes were finished,
On their verandahs they could stand,
And call out to each other
Across the water and the sand.

One day the clouds grew blacker,
Rain thundered from the skies.
It teemed and poured and pelted—
Then the creek began to rise!

The creek became a river,
And the river roared and ran.
It surged and rushed and rattled—
More a lion than a lamb!

The wind blew through the gum trees,
It whistled and it screamed.
The sort of weather Noah knew—
Or that's the way it seemed!

The creek was like a living thing,
A full-on foaming flood,
A roaring, raging monster
That was out for human blood.

The wind whipped up waves wilder
Than humans ever saw.
Those waves demolished Bluey's house
And smashed it on the shore.

Then though they lashed and crashed about,
Those waves could never reach
Clancy's house upon its rock,
High above the beach.

And when the storm had faded
And the creek had gone back down,
The house built high on solid rock
Was still there—safe and sound.

The Puzzle of the Second Will

~~~><X><~~~

Constable Clancy Paterson, the only policeman in the small outback town of Yallambee, was sitting in the office in the front room of the police cottage, labouring away at the paper work he hated so much, when he heard a knock on the screen door.

'Come in,' he called, pleased by any interruption.

The screen door opened and little old Edith McDonald stepped in. She looked distressed and agitated.

Her hands fluttered in front of her as she said, 'He's going to take my house! I can't believe it! He's going to take my house!'

'Who's going to take your house, Edith?' asked the policeman, and then, before she could answer, he added, 'Come and take a seat. I'll get Matty to make us both a cup of tea and you can tell me all about it.'

Clancy's young wife Matty was only in the next room and she called out, 'I heard that, Clancy—I'll put the kettle on in a moment.'

While they were waiting for the tea to come, Edith explained. 'It's that nephew of mine—Robert Prescott. And we always thought Robert was such a nice boy. And now he's doing this! I just can't believe it!'

'Just go back to the beginning, Edith,' said Clancy, 'and tell me all about it.'

'Well,' said the little old lady, drawing a deep breath, 'as you know, Clancy, it was just about a month ago that my dear brother Harold passed away. Oh, yes, of course you know—you and dear Matty were at the funeral. Anyway, after living together in the old family house for so many years, and nursing Harold though his final illness, I always believed that I would inherit the house. I know that it passed to Harold alone under Papa's will, but Harold always said that he'd leave it to me. And more than that, Clancy, he showed me the will—I saw in writing that he was leaving me the house. That's the will that's lodged with our solicitors in Wongalla. But now Robert has turned up with *another* will . . .'

'Another will?' responded the policeman, puzzled.

'A second will,' explained Edith as Matty arrived and served the tea. 'Robert says that it's a later will, and so it replaces the earlier will, and he showed it to me . . . and . . . oh, dear me . . . it really does say that the house and land go to Robert, not me. I just don't understand it. Harold would never have done anything like that—not without telling me.'

Edith and Clancy drank their tea, and then Clancy offered to walk her back to the old family house—the house down beside Wallaby Creek that was at issue in the disputed will.

As they walked through the blazing heat of mid-afternoon in the small outback town, Edith said, 'I'm not even sure this is a police matter, Clancy—so it's very kind of you to come. Robert's at the house now, with the new will. Perhaps if you looked at it, and talked to Robert, you might be able to explain to me just where I stand.'

Clancy promised to do his best while inwardly cursing the young nephew who was putting this sweet old lady through so much distress.

When Clancy and Edith arrived at the sprawling timber bungalow they found the nephew, Robert, sitting on the front verandah in a cane chair reading the newspaper.

He greeted them in a friendly way, and Clancy explained that he was here because of Miss McDonald's distress over the new will that Robert had produced.

'I do feel terribly sorry for dear old Aunt Edith,' Robert said in a slimy way, 'but the law's the law. A new will replaces an older one, and in the new will Uncle Harold left the property to me. And I would let Aunt Edith stay here for the rest of her life, but I'm afraid I just can't afford to. I have creditors pressing me, you see, so I'll have to put this place on the market.'

'Can I see the new will please?' asked Clancy.

'Certainly, officer,' replied Robert, who ducked inside the house and returned with a sheet of paper.

'As you can see, Uncle Harold drew this up himself without a solicitor, but he knew the proper way to do it, and it's all in order and signed and witnessed and so on.'

Clancy turned to Edith and said, 'Is this Harold's handwriting?'

'I suppose so,' said the old lady in a small voice. 'It's a bit shaky, but then his hands were shaky towards the end.'

'So,' said Clancy, 'it might have been written by Harold when he was ill, or it might be a clever forgery.'

Robert began to splutter and protest, but Clancy cut him short. 'Where did you find this will?'

'Exactly where Uncle Robert told me to look for it. He told me, during one of my visits, that he was drawing up a new will, and he'd leave it for me in the family Bible. He told me just where to look—in the book of Psalms, between pages 791 and 792. And when he passed away I went to the bookshelf in his room, took down the family Bible, and looked where he'd told me to look—in the book of Psalms, between pages 791 and 792. And sure enough, there it was, the new will—the one you have in your hand now.'

Clancy Paterson slowly smiled as he said, 'Robert, my lad, you're a liar. And that means that this will is almost certainly forgery. And you've just condemned yourself out of your own mouth.'

What has Robert said that proves that he's a liar and that the will is almost certainly a forgery? (Solution at the end of the next yarn.)

Good Old Uncle George!

Young Chris Anderson was a fan of classical music. But since he lived in a small outback town he rarely had a chance to go to a concert and hear a symphony orchestra or any of the world's great classical musicians.

Chris worked with his mum and dad on the family farm. Of course, he had a collection of CDs and quite a good hi fi system, but still it wasn't the same as the real thing—sitting in a great concert hall, listening to a great orchestra and a great soloist.

One day an envelope arrived at the farm addressed to Chris. When he opened it he found inside a letter from his Uncle George (his mother's brother) and some tickets.

'Dear Chris,' said the letter. 'I know how much you love that high brow music stuff of yours, and I know you really miss getting to the big concerts and all that sort of thing, so I've bought you a set of four tickets to four concerts that I think you might like. I've also booked you into a five-star hotel not far from the Sydney Opera House for a couple of weeks in November so you can go to the concerts. And I've even booked the airfares to take you to Sydney and back.'

Having read this far, Chris shook the tickets out of the envelope and looked at them. They were tickets for a series of four concerts at the Sydney Opera House in November in which one of the world's greatest violinists, Vladimir Ashkenazy, together with the Sydney Symphony

Orchestra, would be playing the works of Sibelius. There was also a letter from a top hotel saying that his bookings for the dates concerned had been made and paid for. And the necessary airline tickets.

Chris blinked in astonishment—he simply couldn't believe it. It was too good to be true. Then he went back to the letter and read the rest of what Uncle George had written.

'I reckon,' said Uncle George in the letter, 'that you deserve a treat. You've been working away like Jacky on that farm, looking after your mum and dad, without a word of complaint, for ten years now. So this is just my way of saying "thank you" and "well done", young Chris. Hope you enjoy yourself. Signed, Uncle George.'

Chris rushed into the kitchen and read the letter to his mum.

'Isn't that nice,' she said as she continued cutting up the beans.

'But is it true?' asked Chris. 'Uncle George has never done anything like this for me before. I just can't believe it's true.'

'Why wouldn't it be true?' his mother asked.

'Well,' replied Chris, 'Uncle George is not exactly made of money, and this would have cost quite a packet.'

'Maybe he's been saving,' said his mum, not looking up from the sink.

'Why would he spend the money on me?' asked Chris.

'Why not?' replied mum. 'You always were his favourite, and he doesn't have any kids of his own. Your Uncle George is not a practical joker, and that certainly looks like his handwriting. So you need to work out if you trust your Uncle George to tell the truth or not. And if you trust Uncle George—then it's good news.'

Moral: Confident trust depends on trustworthiness.

The Bible says: 'I write these things to you who believe in the name of the Son of God that you may know that you have eternal life' (1 John 5:13).

What must a person do to have eternal life? The answer: believe in the Son of God. The word 'believe' here means 'trust', and the 'Son of God' is Jesus. In other words, we can be assured (we can know!) that we have eternal life if we are trusting in the utterly trustworthy one: Jesus.

Solution to 'The Puzzle of the Second Will'

The problem is in the place where Robert claimed he found the new will—in the family Bible, in the book of Psalms, between pages 791 and 792. That is impossible, because odd numbered pages in books are *always* right hand pages, and even numbered pages are *always* left hand pages. That means that pages 791 and 792 would have been the front and back of the same page—and nothing could have been hidden between those two numbers.

The moral from this mystery: When you try to take something out of the Bible that wasn't there in the first place, what you end up with is a lie.

Robert claimed to have got something out of the family Bible that could never have been in there—certainly not in the place where he said it was. And what he produced was a lie: 'When you try to take something out of the Bible that wasn't there in the first place, what you end up with is a lie.'

For instance, some people say that God wants them to be happy. They claim to find this in the Bible. This is the sort of thing the businessman says who's about to leave his wife and live with his secretary: 'God wants me to be happy.' But the Bible doesn't say that. The Bible never says God wants you to be happy—but rather that God wants you to be holy. What the Bible promises is hardship in this world, happiness in heaven, and holiness as the goal in both: 'When you try to take something out of the Bible that wasn't there in the first place, what you end up with is a lie.'

'What the prophets said is true. So you should pay close attention to their message, as you would to a lamp shining in some dark place . . . The prophets did not think these things up on their own, but they were guided by the Spirit of God' (2 Peter 1:19–21 CEV).

Digger's Luck

(Luke 12:16–21)

Digger Jones was a prospector,
And he had been all his life.
He had worked hard and he'd struggled
To support his kids and wife.

At Lightning Ridge he'd dug for opals,
Panned for gold at Sovereign Hill,
He'd fossicked in the blazing sun,
Worked at it with a will.

Then one day outside Kalgoorlie,
As he choked upon the dust,
He found what he had dreamed about
As he'd struggled for a crust.

The nugget that his shovel struck
Made him wobbly in the legs:
It was the size, he clearly saw,
Of seven emu eggs!

He couldn't quite believe his luck!
Like a jackpot Lotto win!
The message of the nugget was:
'Now your ship's come in!'

As they weighed and assayed it,
And people slapped his back,
Digger planned to switch his life
On to a brand new track.

He planned to make investments
As he said 'goodbye' to cares.
He planned to find security
In lots of stocks and shares.

And then he planned on leisure,
Lots of loafing in the sun,
Round a million dollar mansion—
Lots of lazy sorts of fun!

 'Come on! Drink up!' said Digger,
'Have a beer, or wine, or sherry,
My philosophy,' said Digger, 'is
Eat and drink and just be merry!'

But God said this to Digger:
'You're a boofhead! Drongo! Dill!
Don't you realise death's coming?
You had better make a will!'

On a leisured life of luxury,
Digger's plans were pinned,
But Digger's life was snuffed out—
Like a candle in the wind.

Weep for Digger's faded plan—
The fall of it! The gall of it!
How much did Digger leave behind?
All of it—all of it!

The Puzzle of the Circus Robbery

The circus had come to the outback town of Wongalla. At the nearby smaller township of Yallambee, Matty Paterson asked her husband Clancy, the town's only policeman, to take her to see the show.

'Why not?' replied Clancy. 'It's years since we've been to a circus. And no circus will ever come here to Yallambee—it's too small. Listen, I'll tell you what, Matty love—next Thursday I have to be in Wongalla to make a court appearance (I have to give evidence in that drunk driving matter). So why don't you come with me, and then after the court session is over we can go and have a bite to eat at one of those cafes in Wongalla mall, then go to the circus.'

And so it was agreed.

The following Thursday, when Clancy put on his cleanest uniform and drove the police patrol van from Yallambee across to Wongalla, his young wife was beside him in the passenger's seat.

Matty sat in the public gallery of the police court that afternoon while Clancy gave his evidence. Later they went to the pizza and gelato cafe in the Wongalla mall, and then on to the circus.

It wasn't a big circus, and, truth to tell, not a particularly good one. There was only one elephant in the show. It was ridden by a young woman in spangled tights who performed acrobatic tricks on the elephant's back and was billed as 'Princess Karma'.

One of the troupe of clowns, however, was particularly clever and funny. He had pots and pans and battered old saucepans dangling off his clown suit, and was addressed by the others as 'Biffo'. He banged and bashed his pots and pans as he walked around, finding an endless stream of funny things to do with them.

Finally the show was over, and Clancy and Matty Paterson walked out into the warm night air. Clancy was about to buy Matty some more fairy floss when a man in shirtsleeves came staggering out of a nearby caravan with a saucepan in one hand and clutching the back of his head with the other.

'I've been robbed!' he yelled.

He saw Clancy, who was still in uniform, and bellowed, 'Hey you! Copper! I've been robbed!'

'You want some help, mate?' Clancy asked as the man staggered towards them through the mud around his caravan.

'You bet I do,' growled the man. 'And they say you can never find a copper when you want one. The name's Griffin. I'm the manager of this circus, and I've just been robbed of a week's takings.'

Clancy asked what had happened. Griffin explained that he'd been sitting at his desk doing the books when someone had crept up silently behind him and hit him over the head. When he came to, the cash box was gone.

'What were you hit with?' asked Clancy. 'What weapon was used?'

'This,' responded Griffin, holding up the battered old saucepan in his hand.

'Let's have a look at the scene of the crime,' said Clancy.

Clancy and Matty waded cautiously through the sea of mud that surrounded the manager's caravan. ('It's the animals,' Griffin explained. 'The elephant, the camels and the horses have been around churning up the dirt.') Inside the van Clancy found the place spic and span: everything neatly organised and in its place, with no sign of forced entry. In fact the caravan was immaculate—without a mark anywhere.

'Nothing much to learn here,' said the policeman.

As they descended the steps again, Clancy asked Griffin if there were any witnesses.

'Sure,' called a voice from about ten feet away. 'I saw what happened.'

Clancy turned around and saw the woman billed as Princess Karma, the elephant acrobat.

'So what did you see, Betty?' asked Griffin. (Ah, thought Clancy, Princess Karma's real name is Betty.)

'I saw Rex climbing out of your caravan window with the cashbox under his arm.'

Griffin spun around and called out to Biffo the clown. 'Hey, Rex—get over here.' (So, thought Clancy, Biffo's real name is Rex.)

The clown clanked over to face the angry manager, who yelled, 'Did you hit me over the head and steal the cash box?'

'Of course not,' said Rex with a look of hurt innocence behind his clown's make-up.

'I always leave the caravan window open behind me when I'm working at the desk,' said Griffin. 'Everyone knows that. Are you sure you didn't climb in, hit me and steal the money?'

'I told you, didn't I?' responded Rex. 'Anyway,' he added, 'it's Betty here who plays the horses, not me. I saw you, Betty, paying off that bookie after the show.'

'So I had a couple of bob on the daily double. So what?' sneered Betty.

Then Griffin turned to Clancy Paterson and said, 'Can you make any sense of this? Who attacked me and stole the cash box?'

'Well,' said Clancy, 'I'd like you to hold Betty here—Princess Karma or whatever she's called—while I call the Wongalla police station. Once she's under arrest we'll find out who her bookmaker is and see if any of the money can be recovered.'

'You don't have anything on me,' protested Betty.

'Actually, sister,' said Clancy, 'there are four clues that point to your guilt.'

What are those four clues? How many of them can you pick up? (Solution at the end of the next yarn.)

Green and Growing

In one corner of the home yard, not far from the farmhouse, there grew an apple tree. Truth to tell, as Dave Rudd used to say, it was a sorry excuse for an apple tree. The tree itself was small and stunted, and it rarely produced any fruit. And when it did finally produce the occasional apple it was small, sour and useless.

Dave was standing in front of the tree one day with his hands on his hips and a disgusted expression on his face.

'Dad,' he said at last after a long silence, 'it's time to pull this tree out and chuck it on the fire.'

'Why do you say that, Dave?' responded Dad Rudd from his cane chair on the farmhouse verandah.

'It's useless,' explained Dave. 'This tree was planted for the purpose of giving us apples—and it never gives us anything worthwhile. All we get is occasional, useless, shrivelled up, sour fruit. It doesn't give us what it's meant to give us. It's a waste of space.'

'So then, Dave, what do you want to do?'

'Chop it down and cut it up for firewood. That's about the only thing it's good for.'

'I have a suggestion for you, Dave,' said Dad. 'If you want to get more out of this tree, the first step is to give more to the tree.'

'Eh?' said Dave, his eyebrows climbing up his forehead. 'I don't follow. Whadda ya mean?'

'I mean,' said Dad patiently, 'that instead of chopping

the thing down you should try watering it regularly. Give it a really generous drink every day. And feed it. Dig all around its roots and give it a good feed of fertiliser every week. Keep this up for months, not just a week or two, and see what happens then.'

So Dave did as his Dad suggested.

The result was quite remarkable. The tree put out new shoots. Soon it started to grow taller and stronger. And when it was fruit season, it produced a crop of large, sweet apples.

Dave discovered that the more he gave to the tree, the more the tree gave to him.

Moral: Generosity feeds and breeds generosity.

The Bible says: 'Grow in the grace and knowledge of our Lord and Saviour Jesus Christ' (2 Peter 3:18).

This word 'grace' means 'generosity'—and not just ordinary, everyday generosity, but amazing, astonishing, over-the-top, mind-blowing generosity. That's what God offers his people—the continual, daily experience of his astonishing generosity. And the more of his generosity we experience the more generous we will be to those around us: generosity feeds and breeds generosity.

Being Christian doesn't mean standing still, or just jogging along in the same old way all the time. Being Christian means growing. But how do we grow? We grow by 'Growing in the grace and knowledge of our Lord and Saviour Jesus Christ'.

The Bible is real food. By feeding on that we grow in the knowledge of Jesus Christ, and we grow in the grace (the astonishing generosity) of Jesus Christ.

Solution to 'The Puzzle of the Circus Robbery'

Here are the four clues that gave Betty the elephant rider away:

1. Rex, a.k.a. Biffo the clown, could never have 'crept up silently' behind Griffin the manager and hit him over the head. All the clanking pots and pans dangling off his clown suit made a dreadful racket. So the accusation against him must be false.

2. Since Betty, a.k.a. Princess Karma, made this false accusation, she must have had a reason to do so—probably to deflect suspicion from herself.

3. We know she was in debt to a bookmaker, and bookies don't come in person to collect a couple of bob bet on the daily double. She must have been seriously in debt to the bookie for him to come to the circus to see her, so she had a motive to commit the crime.

4. The caravan was spic and span with not a mark anywhere—and yet it was surrounded by a sea of mud. How could anyone have attacked Griffin without leaving muddy tracks on the caravan's floor? Clancy knew there was one possible answer: that Betty rode up to the open window on the back of her elephant and threw the saucepan at the back of Griffin's head as he sat at his desk with his back to the window. When this knocked him unconscious, she reached in through the window and stole the cashbox. She used a battered old saucepan as the weapon in a further attempt to throw suspicion onto Rex.

The moral from this mystery: 'What were you thinking!'

Have you ever seen Dr Phil on television? Dr Phil is a Texan and a pop-psychologist who has a talk show in which he advises people on their problems. He is famous for certain little sayings or slogans. One of these is: 'What were you thinking!' When someone appears on his show who has done something really stupid, Dr Phil cries out in despair: 'What were you thinking!'

That's what should be said to Betty the elephant rider. The robbery and the story she told to implicate Rex the clown were so stupid that all one could say in response was: 'What were you thinking!'

And there are times when that is exactly what I want to say to those people who think they can get away with living their lives ignoring God. I want to cry out in frustration: 'What are you thinking!'

Do they really think God is so stupid he won't notice what they're up to? Do they really think they can hide or excuse their wrongdoings, failures and failings from God himself?

The Bible says: 'each person dies only once and after that comes judgment' (Hebrews 9:27 NLT). At that judgment, do these people really think God won't know what has actually gone on inside their lives, and inside their minds? What *are* they thinking! An ounce of intelligence would tell them they won't get away with that.

But if we *do* stop and think, if we come to our senses and investigate a bit, we find that there *is* a way to survive God's judgment. Here's the rest of that quote from the Bible: 'Just as it is destined that each person dies only once and after that comes judgment, so also Christ died only once as a sacrifice to take away the sins of many people' (Hebrews 9:27–28 NLT). And that means he can take away your sins, and mine.

Stop and think. Come to your senses. Accept the gift of forgiveness that Jesus has paid for and that Jesus offers.

The Squatter and the Swaggie

(Luke 16:19–23)

There was a wealthy squatter
Simply rolling in the dough.
All his ancestors before him
Had been wealthy so-and-so's.

He wore his moleskins and his boots,
As made by R.M. Williams;
He wore his coat of Harris Tweed
That made him look a million!

Though his sheep and cattle station
Was at least ten thousand acres,
He hated feeding swaggies,
Called them 'Lazy, lousy fakers'.

Lying at his homestead gate
Was a sickly, older swaggie,
Who was looking pale and poorly
And quite positively daggy.

As he leaned against the gatepost,
His swag all torn and tattered,
He said: 'I'm feeling awful crook,
And old, and tired, and battered.'

The swagman (name of Larry),
As he lay there thought: 'Perhaps
If the squatter has a banquet
Then at least I'll get the scraps.'

As the sickly swaggie lay there,
He spent his time in prayer.
But Sir William 'Wealthy Squatter'
Didn't pray—he didn't care.

The station dogs came sniffing round,
The swaggie counted seven,
And then he fell asleep—and woke
To find himself—in heaven!

Meanwhile, the wealthy squatter
Ate his foods all fat and fried,
Until his arteries closed up
And the squatter also died.

The squatter had a funeral
That was positively flash.
The VIPs all came along
To show respect for all that cash!

But the squatter found himself
In Outer Darkness . . . feeling needy.
'I hate this place,' he sadly said,
'It's hot as Coober Pedy!'

And then he glimpsed the swaggie,
In a place that looked real nice.
'Oy!' yelled out the squatter,
'You there! In paradise!'

'I'm here frying in the darkness
While I guess you've got it made.
Can't you send me down a little help?
Say, a nice cool lemonade?'

'There's a chasm fixed between us,'
Were the words of the reply.
'You should have prayed before you died,
Now's too late, don't even try.'

'Please listen,' said the squatter,
'To one last request I'll make:
Could Larry Swaggie please go back
And warn my folks, for goodness' sake?

'I have, you see, five brothers—
At the homestead they are gathered.
They mustn't end up where I am,
That's what really matters.'

The reply that came from heaven
Said: 'Your brothers have the Bible.
That's the book in which God speaks,
It's both truthful and reliable.'

'No! No!' called out the squatter
From his place of dark despair,
'They'll all ignore the Bible,
They won't think to find truth there.

'But if someone from the dead comes back
Then they'll know the score.'
The sad reply from heaven said:
'They won't listen any more.

'Their hearts are hard, their minds are fixed,
On selfish insurrection;
And they ignore the evidence
Of historic resurrection.'

The Puzzle of the Hit and Run

Constable Clancy Paterson and his young wife Matty were eating lunch in the kitchen of the police cottage when the telephone rang.

Clancy spoke briefly to the caller then hung up and said to his wife, 'I've got to go out, Matty. There's been a hit and run accident down the road. The young Butler boy's been hurt.'

Clancy slapped his old blue police-issue Akubra on his head and hurried out the front door. He trotted quickly down the street to where he saw a small crowd gathered. The crowd parted as he arrived, and he saw the town's one and only GP, Doc Moran, crouched over the figure of a small boy lying on the road. Over the doctor's shoulder Clancy could see the freckled face and red hair of ten-year-old Josh Butler.

'How is he, Doc?' asked the policeman.

'Nothing's broken,' replied the medical man, rising to his feet. 'And there are no signs of internal injuries. He's got a few cuts, scratches and bruises, and he's in shock at the moment. My best guess is he'll be fine. But you can't be too careful in these cases, so I've had someone call the ambulance from Wongalla. They can do some X-rays at the Base Hospital, and probably keep him in overnight for observation.'

Clancy muttered quietly, 'It could have been worse, I guess.'

'It could have been a lot worse,' agreed the doctor. 'From what I've heard, the boy could have been killed.'

Just then young Josh's mum arrived, knelt down and stroked his hair, and the doctor had to repeat his report on the boy's condition and likely prospects. While this was going on, Clancy spoke to the crowd.

'Who saw it happen?' he asked.

Silence was the only reply, so he continued. 'Then who was the first here, on the spot?'

Clarissa Milburn, the hairdresser, spoke up. 'That would have been me, Clancy,' she said.

'All right then, Clarissa,' said the policeman, 'just tell me what you saw.'

'I come out because I heard a thump and a bit of a squeal, like. When I got out the front door of the shop the street was deserted. Wasn't a single soul in sight—just little Josh there, flat on his back on the road.'

'Did you see the car?'

'It was almost around the corner, but I saw it all right.'

Clancy raised one eyebrow and waited for her go on. In a township as small as Yallambee most people knew everybody else's cars.

Somewhat reluctantly Clarissa said, 'I'm pretty sure it was Ralph Logan's car—an old white Valiant. And I think it must have been Ralph at the wheel. It was certainly a big bloke—tall, broad shoulders, just like Ralph.'

A short while later the ambulance arrived, and the young accident victim and his mum left for the hospital. Clancy took Clarissa back to the police cottage where he took a statement from her. Then he got into the police patrol van and drove out to Ralph Logan's property, just north of town.

Driving onto the property he noticed a fresh scrape on the wooden gatepost—a large slash of white timber showed where a piece of wood had been chipped off by a bump from a passing vehicle.

In the front yard of the homestead he saw Ralph Logan's old white Valiant. One side mudguard had been pushed in and paint scraped off. He bent down and examined the damage for a minute or two, and then mounted the verandah and entered the open front door, calling out 'G'day—anyone in?' as he did so.

Clancy found Ralph Logan and his wife Kathy in the kitchen with a freshly made pot of tea. He accepted the offer of a cup and then told them about the hit and run accident involving young Josh. They both wanted to know about the boy's condition, so Clancy relieved their minds by telling them the good news.

Then he said, 'Now, Ralph—a witness has identified your car as being the vehicle that knocked young Josh down and then drove off.'

'Well, it wasn't me, Clancy,' said Ralph. 'You can forget that idea for a start. I wasn't in town today, was I love?' he added, appealing to his wife.

She nodded in agreement, but said nothing.

'My witness told me,' resumed Clancy, 'that you were at the wheel. It was a big bloke, she said.'

'Ah, well that can't be right,' insisted Ralph. 'I haven't driven the car for days. Kath was the last one who drove it, when she ran over to Wongalla a couple of days ago.'

Again Kathy Logan nodded in agreement, and then poured herself a second cup of tea.

'Look here,' continued Ralph, 'no one could mistake me and Kath, could they?' He gestured at his wife, who was a tiny woman—little more than five feet tall. 'So if they said they saw a big bloke at the wheel it couldn't have been Kath—and it couldn't have been me because I haven't driven the car for days.'

Clancy said, 'I noticed the damage to the front wing of your car, Ralph, when I passed it in the yard. Had a bit of a bingle?'

'Ah, yeah,' said the farmer, looking sheepish. 'I wasn't real careful and collected the gatepost four or five nights back.'

'That dint looks serious to me,' continued the policeman. 'Surely it's rubbing against the tyre? I'm not dead certain I'd pass that car as roadworthy, Ralph, with that dint in it.'

'But it's *not* rubbing on the tyre,' insisted the big man. 'Come on outside and I'll show you.'

Out in the front yard Ralph jumped into his car, started the engine immediately, and drove the vehicle around in a circle. Then he stopped and got out.

'See, see,' he said, 'the tyre's not rubbing—it's perfectly okay.'

'No, it's not, Ralph,' said Clancy quietly. 'You've just shown me that you were the one who ran down young Josh Butler and then failed to stop.'

How does Clancy know this? What piece of evidence has revealed the truth? (Solution at the end of the next yarn.)

On Track

Paddy was on old bushman who knew the bush and knew its ways, and he had travelled over a great deal of Australia for many years. He'd worked in the outback and hiked through the bush, and there wasn't much about travelling rough, or reading the ground, or coping in the bush that old Paddy didn't know.

When his nephews, Colin and Pete (the twins), finished their end-of-high-school exams, Paddy offered to take them on a long bush walk as an excursion—if they wanted to. Well, they did want to. It sounded like an adventure of the first order: hiking for a week or more through the bush in the Snowy Mountains with Uncle Paddy.

They travelled by train down to Jindabyne, and from there they set out, all three with heavy packs on their backs. Paddy led them up into the high valleys and deep bush. He knew his bush tucker and was able to point out the fruits and plants that were edible. For the first two days they heated up canned food over their camp fires, but on the third day they came across a fast-flowing, icy cold mountain stream. They dropped in fishing lines and caught several big trout. That night they had a real feast.

In the morning they swam and washed in the icy waters, and then they set out again. By this time Colin and Pete were starting to feel pretty confident. They'd been watching old Paddy and learning his bush tricks, and they thought their own survival skills were now pretty good. Besides which, as Colin reminded Pete, they were not complete amateurs. They'd often been on bushwalking and camping trips with their school. They knew their way about, and each wanted to take a turn at guiding their little group.

Uncle Paddy wasn't so sure this was a good idea.

'I know this country, boys,' he said. 'I know a lot of this place like the back of my hand. I've been around here for years. It might be simpler if I do the guiding and pick the paths we take.'

'But that's not fair, Uncle Paddy,' complained Colin. Pete joined in and said the same thing.

'Now look,' said Paddy firmly, 'your mum and dad have entrusted you to my care. I'm looking after you and that's it. End of discussion.'

For the next few hours Colin and Pete trudged along behind Paddy, feeling resentful, quietly smouldering and becoming more and more rebellious.

Finally, when they stopped for lunch, the two boys had a whispered conversation, then said, 'Which way are you going after lunch, Uncle Paddy?'

'Up towards that ridge,' replied their uncle with a nod of his head.

'Well, you can go that way if you want,' said Colin with a sneer, 'but Pete and I are heading off down towards that valley, between those two cliffs. We know what we're doing, and that's the way we've decided to go. We're leading from now on, Uncle Paddy. And you can either come with us or push off on your own—we don't care which.'

Paddy was most unhappy about this rebellion by his two young charges, but they wouldn't listen to a word he said. When lunch was over and the campfire had been properly extinguished, Paddy once again asked them not to be so foolish, but they laughed at him and said it was *their* excursion, *their* hiking holiday, and they'd go whichever way *they* wanted.

Without waiting for Paddy to say any more, the two boys set off along the lower path that led between two towering cliffs. Because he was responsible for them, Paddy had no choice but to fall into line and follow in their footsteps—if only to keep an eye on them and protect them from harm.

They walked all afternoon until at last, hot and tired, Colin (who was in the lead) pushed aside a thick clump of bushes and found their way blocked by a rock fall. Paddy sat down and waited until the two boys had discovered there was no way around the rock fall in that narrow valley and they would have to go back to where they had been that morning and start off again.

'I could have told you this valley was a dead end . . .' began Uncle Paddy.

'Then why didn't you?' snapped Pete angrily. 'Why didn't you say something at lunchtime instead of letting us spend hours going down the wrong path?'

'I did try. You seem to have forgotten that you inter-rupted me every time I opened my mouth,' responded Paddy.

The next day Pete took the lead. Again refusing to follow Paddy's directions, he insisted they take the track beside the creek. This ended in an unpassable tangle of bush and undergrowth, and once more they had to retrace their steps. Finally they agreed to take the path up the valley side originally suggested by Paddy, but still they refused to allow him to take the lead, and were saved from dangerous falls only because Paddy was watching them closely and called out from the rear of the little group whenever one of them looked like putting a foot wrong.

Colin and Pete came to resent Uncle Paddy more and more over the rest of that week. They were clever, strong young men. They didn't want their old uncle, the weather-beaten old bushie, telling them what to do. In fact, they didn't like *anyone* telling them what to do. So they kept going wrong, kept getting into trouble, kept facing unnec-essary dangers and risks.

But they still made up their own minds, and still refused to listen to Uncle Paddy.

And many people are just as stupid as that when it comes to listening to God. But the Bible says: 'In all your ways acknowledge him, and he will direct your paths' (Proverbs 3:6 NKJV).

Solution to 'The Puzzle of the Hit and Run'

Clancy had noticed that Ralph had been able to leap into the car, start it up and drive it immediately—without adjusting the seat. If Ralph's tiny wife Kathy had been the last to drive the car, Ralph would not have been able to get in and drive it without sliding the seat back to give his larger frame room. That proved he'd lied about not driving the car for two days.

Clancy also suspected the dint in the mudguard was a cover up. Ralph had deliberately hit the gatepost on the way in, to try to hide the dint caused when he ran into the boy. But the mark on the gate was brand new, still showing white timber, so it couldn't have been made four or five nights ago as Ralph claimed.

Faced with these facts, Ralph Logan admitted the truth.

The moral from this mystery: We cannot avoid responsibility for our actions.

Jesus said: 'I tell you, on the day of judgment people will give account for every careless word they speak' (Matthew 12:36).

Middleton's Overseer

(Matthew 18:21–35)

Middleton was a squatter
With a sheep and cattle station.
And on his thousand acres
He was helping to build a nation.

Middleton balanced up his books
At the end of five good years.
He settled the debts of his workers—
The men of stock-whip and shears.

One man owed Middleton heaps of dough,
A debtor without a peer.
This man who owed the largest amount
Was Cleary, the overseer.

'Ten thousand pound!' said Middleton,
Confronting his overseer.
Cleary went pale and shuffled his feet,
And said: 'I had no idea.'

'Well, can you pay? Or can't you?'
Is what the squatter asked.
'Ten thousand pounds I cannot pay,'
Said Cleary, 'A hopeless task.'

'Well, I'm seizing all your property,
To get my money back!'
Middleton said to his overseer,
His expression thunderous and black.

Cleary fell upon his knees
And tears trickled down his face.
'Please give me a few more years to pay!
Please don't take my place!'

Now Middleton was a generous man,
And the seasons had been quite good,
So he took his pen to his ledger book
And crossed out the debt where it stood.

Middleton shared the bounty
Of good prices and seasons fair.
Cleary walked out of the homestead
With a heart as light as air.

Then Cleary spotted a younger man,
Tall and freckled and sandy.
This was Middleton's rouseabout,
A country lad named Andy.

Grabbing him by the collar,
Cleary started to shout:
'You still owe me ten quid, lad!
You layabout rouseabout!'

'Pay your debt!' snarled Cleary,
In his voice was a threatening note,
As Cleary grabbed young Andy
And shook him warmly by the throat!

'Please, Mr Cleary,' said Andy,
'Just give me some time to pay.'
'No! I'll take your horse in payment,'
Said Cleary, 'I'll take it off you today.'

Middleton's other station hands
All heard what Cleary had said.
The words they heard made them hopping mad,
And made them all see red.

They went and reported to their boss
The things they had seen and heard.
They described Mr Cleary's behaviour,
And reported his every word.

Middleton sent for Cleary
And confronted his overseer.
'You are a selfish, wicked man,'
Said Middleton, 'That's now clear.

'I'm reviving your debt and taking your goods,'
Said the boss. 'It's your own stupid fault.
On top of which,' added Middleton,
'I'm having you jailed for assault!'

Cleary had to face up to his judgment,
Just like flour must go through a sieve.
Cleary was judged to be guilty because
He had failed to learn how to forgive!

The Puzzle of the Mouse Mania

Constable Clancy Paterson and his wife Matty ran into young Bobby Scott during the week, shopping with his mother after school in Yallambee's one main street.

Bobby insisted that Clancy come out to their property to see his 'moustarium', as he called it. His mother, Irene, gave in to her son's enthusiasm by inviting Clancy and Matty to lunch on Saturday at their homestead. So the following Saturday saw the Patersons driving out to One Tree station to keep their appointment, and to see Bobby's mysterious 'moustarium'.

As soon as they pulled up in the front yard Bobby insisted on dragging Clancy away. He led the policeman to what looked like an old disused hay shed some distance from the house.

Inside Clancy was amazed to see that Bobby had cleaned the place up and fitted it with benches, boxes and cages. These were filled with mice. There must have been a hundred small rodents living in a complex inter-connecting set of boxes and cages that Bobby called his 'mice city' or moustarium.

'I'm very impressed,' said Clancy, and it was clear that he meant it.

Bobby beamed with delight and said, 'I built all of it myself.'

'All of it?'

'Well . . . most of it. Dad helped a bit. And Mike from next door came and helped. He's breeding mice too.' The place Bobby Scott called 'next door' was, in fact, kilometres away—Nevertire sheep station. And the 'Mike' he mentioned was Mike Evans, the son of the manager of Nevertire.

'Where did this craze for mice come from?' asked Clancy.

'When we had the mice plague last year,' explained Bobby, 'I caught a few of the field mice, put them in a cage and started breeding them. I got real interested and borrowed books from the library and read all about them. Then I started my own breeding program—you know, keeping a record of what colours I could breed from which mice.'

'Just like your father does with his stud sheep?'

'That's right, Mr Paterson. Dad showed me how to keep a breeder's book. Anyway, I started getting these mice of a beautiful golden brown colour, and I decided to enter them in the Wongalla Show later in the year, in the prize pet competition. When I showed them to my mates some of them got interested and started breeding mice too. I had lots by then, so I let them have some of my breeding stock.'

'Including young Mike from next door?'

'That's right. Now, let me show you this one here, Mr Paterson . . . '

The next half hour was taken up with Bobby showing Clancy the best mice in his collection. Then Irene Scott called them from the homestead verandah and they went in to lunch.

Over the meal Bobby's father, Ted, said that sometimes he worried he was indulging the boy too much. But Irene interrupted and said, 'Nonsense. This thing with the mice is encouraging him to take an interest in the science of breeding, and encouraging him to show a bit of enterprise. It's good for him.'

Clancy explained the size and ambition of Bobby's

project to Matty, who agreed that it was good for a school boy to take on a project he was responsible for.

'At the same time,' added Irene, 'I must admit that it sometimes gives me the creeps to think of the number of mice running around inside all those boxes in the old hay shed.'

'And when I think,' added Bobby's father, 'that it started with wild mice from the thousands we were killing last year—oh boy, I don't like those little things. When they come in plague proportions they do an awful lot of damage. But as long as they stay in their cages I won't blow my top.'

Just as they were finishing lunch, a ute pulled up in front of the homestead and young Mike Evans and his father Barry from Nevertire got out. Barry came into to say 'G'day' and talk to Ted about the fat stock sales coming up.

Mike pulled a huge piece of cheese out of his pocket and offered to go to the shed and feed Bobby's mice. Bobby agreed enthusiastically and the two boys ran off. Clancy was about to say something to them, but they disappeared in a cloud of dust before he could open his mouth. And then he was distracted by being offered another cup of tea and a yarn with Ted and Barry.

The next day Clancy received a distressed telephone call from young Bobby saying that half his mice were dead.

'They must have been poisoned, Mr Paterson,' he said tearfully. 'Otherwise, how come so many of them died at once? And all my best breeders have died too. It's a mouse poisoning case, Mr Paterson—will you come out and investigate?'

Clancy Paterson smiled to himself, and then said seriously, 'There's no need for that, Bobby—I think I can tell you exactly what happened to your mice.'

What has happened to Bobby Scott's mice? And how does Clancy know? (Solution at the end of the next yarn.)

The 'Open Pocket' Pattern

Frank Chambers was born on a sprawling sheep station in the western district. It was a wealthy property that specialised in breeding stud rams and ewes. As a young man Frank travelled in Africa, and in the city of Nairobi he was horrified by the poverty and sickness, the terrible living conditions, and the high infant mortality rate among the slum dwellers.

Frank decided to do something about it—to use his wealth to make a difference. He contacted the Church Missionary Society and offered to personally sponsor and pay for a Christian medical clinic in the Nairobi slums.

In due course the clinic was set up and did a great deal of good.

As the years passed Frank's father died, and Frank inherited the family property. He settled down to manage the stud sheep business, married and raised his family. Frank had only one son, a boy named Roger.

Throughout his childhood years Roger came to understand that the great passion of his father's life was the Christian medical clinic in Africa. Over time it grew, and a whole chain of these clinics were set up in the swarming, overcrowded slums of Nairobi. The good they did was immeasurable.

All of this Frank Chambers funded from his own pocket. Every year or two he would take a holiday in Africa so that he could visit the clinics, encourage the staff and see what was happening for himself. As Roger grew older Frank took him along on these trips. Roger could see just how valuable and worthwhile this work was.

Roger had no heart for farming, but he was a clever student, and at the end of high school he announced that he wanted to study law. Frank supported him in this, paid for him to attend university, and gave him a weekly allowance to provide for his living expenses.

It was while he was a student that Roger suddenly realised one day how much he owed his father. He had inherited his intelligence and good health from Frank, and his father had paid for all his needs and encouraged and supported him in everything he did. Roger decided that one way of responding to his father's care and generosity was to generously support the project that mattered most to him: the Christian medical clinics in Nairobi.

Even as a student, if Roger had any money to spare he would send it to the Church Missionary Society earmarked for those clinics.

After he graduated and became a successful and well-to-do lawyer, Roger regularly gave as much as he could to support them—because he realised that his own wealth, his own success, grew out of what his father had invested in him. Supporting what was dear to his father's heart was one way of properly acknowledging this.

Moral: God has been generous to us, and we should respond by being generous to God.

The Bible says: 'On the first day of every week, each of you should set aside a sum of money in keeping with his income' (1 Corinthians 16:2 NIV).

Solution to 'The Puzzle of the Mouse Mania'

In a way the mice *had* been poisoned—but by accident. It was the cheese that did it.

These were wild mice, or field mice, that were used to living on a diet of seeds and grain. When they were in plague proportions they would eat almost anything—but cheese was still not good for them. A thousand mice and more can be fed oats, wheat, milk, bread, raw eggs and many other things quite safely—but not cheese. Cheese overheats their blood!

The moral from this mystery: We can be wrong about what's good for us and what's bad for us.

Both Bobby Scott and Mike Evans thought that cheese would be good for the mice (perhaps they'd watched too many Tom and Jerry cartoons!). They meant well, but they were mistaken. What they thought would be good for the mice ended up killing many of them.

In much the same way, what we think is good for us can end up killing us. Jesus said: 'Do not lay up for yourselves treasures on earth, where moth and rust destroy and where thieves break in and steal, but lay up for yourselves treasures in heaven, where neither moth nor rust destroys and where thieves do not break in and steal. For where your treasure is, there your heart will be also' (Matthew 6:19-21).

The Missing Merino

(Luke 15:3–7)

Just outside Snake Gully,
On Jindawarra Station,
Harrison, the owner,
Suffered aggravation.

He knew how many sheep he owned,
He knew what the number should be,
He expected his station hands to count
One thousand, five hundred and three.

But when they counted all the sheep,
Each ram, and lamb, and ewe,
The total that they counted was . . .
One thousand, five hundred and two!

'What's happened to me missing sheep?
Where could the blighter have gone?'
Said Harrison as he mounted up,
'I'll search the hills—and beyond.'

He left the station hands in charge
Of the sheep back in the home yard.
As he left, he said to his leading hand:
'Look after this mob—stand guard.'

Harrison searched the distant paddocks,
Each gully and dried up creek.
Until he found that one lost sheep
He knew he'd continue to seek.

But then he heard a faint bleating,
From beside a small billabong.
And there, among the coolabahs,
Was the sheep for which he longed.

He lifted it onto his horse's back
(That sheep that had wanted to roam),
Then climbed back into the saddle and
Turned his horse towards home.

When he got back to the homestead
And the sheep was back on it feet,
Harrison said: 'Let's celebrate
The fact that the flock is complete!'

The Puzzle of the Midnight Visitor

Constable Clancy Paterson and his young wife Matty were sound asleep. It was a hot night, so they were sleeping with just a sheet over them and with the windows of their bedroom wide open. But the night was still as well as hot, and there was barely a breath of air coming in through the flyscreens that covered the windows.

Down the dark hallway from their bedroom, the kitchen clock ticked loudly and then chimed midnight. Just a few minutes later the telephone beside the bed began to ring.

Clancy grabbed it and mumbled, 'Yeah, police station—what's up?'

'Clancy, is that you?' asked a shaky voice.

Clancy forced himself to sit up in bed and wake up properly. 'Who else would it be?' he muttered. 'Who's calling?'

'It's me,' came the reply, 'Stan McPherson—out at Dagworth station. I've just got back from Sydney and found that I've been robbed. The place has been ransacked and my nephew, Steve Riley, who was looking after the place for me, has been assaulted. Can you come out?'

'I'll be there as soon as I can,' replied the policeman. He hung up the phone and turned on the bedside lamp. Matty opened one eye and murmured, 'What is it?'

'Stan McPherson's been robbed,' explained her

husband as he grabbed his uniform from the chair beside the bed.

'Poor Stan,' said Matty, then rolled over and went back to sleep.

Clancy backed the police patrol van out of his backyard and drove down the wide, deserted main street of Yallambee. From the vehicle radio he called into the district police headquarters at Wongalla to report the suspected break and enter, and that he was attending the scene.

Then he was barrelling down the dusty gravel road that led to Dagworth sheep station. But he had to watch his speed because even on high beam his headlights gave only a limited view of the road ahead, and at any moment an animal might come bounding out of the bush and cause him to slam on the brakes. The air was still hot and oppressive, and he drove with the windows open.

When the constable arrived at Dagworth, Stan was standing out the front of the house, a can of beer in his hand, looking down the track and waiting.

'Thanks for coming out at this hour, Clancy,' he said as he showed the policeman inside.

Clancy could see at a glance that the sprawling homestead had indeed been ransacked. Furniture had been pulled out and draws upended.

'What's missing?' asked Paterson, looking at the mess.

'Money,' replied the station owner. 'Appliances. Pieces of my wife's jewellery that we left here when we went to Sydney for our holiday.'

'Where's your wife now, Stan?'

'I left Christina and the two girls in Sydney. They're going to the ballet and some social things. I don't care for that stuff so I came back. I rang Steve and said I was coming back early—told him I'd stop at a motel halfway and get back about midday tomorrow. But I didn't feel tired so I kept on driving—drove all night—got here at midnight and found this.'

Slumped in an armchair and rubbing his eyes was Stan McPherson's nephew Steve Riley.

Clancy pulled out his notebook, flipped it open and said, 'What can you tell me, Steve?'

The story that Steve Riley told was as follows: during the morning, sometime after nine o'clock, there was a knock at the front door. He went to the door and stepped out on the verandah. He could see no one, but he was suddenly grabbed from behind.

'The bloke who grabbed me,' said Steve, 'must have been hiding around the corner of the verandah. Anyway, I put up a struggle, but he had both my arms pinned behind my back. Then some other blokes appeared. Before I knew it I'd been tied up and blindfolded. They led me back into the house, and in the kitchen they forced a pill into my mouth and then forced water down my throat until I swallowed it. It must have been a real strong sleeping pill because I started to feel woozy almost at once. Then they pushed me into the linen cupboard and locked the door.

'After that the pill took effect and I fell asleep. It was pitch black inside that linen cupboard—no light gets in there at all, even in the middle of the day, so that probably helped the pill to knock me out. I must have slept for hours, I guess. When I came to I looked at my luminous watch and saw it was almost midnight. Just then I heard Uncle Stan come back in, and when he saw the mess the house was in he called out my name. I yelled out that I was in the linen cupboard. He unlocked the door and let me out. The thieves are probably miles and miles away by now. Sorry, Uncle Stan, but there was nothing I could do about it.'

'Not your fault, Steve,' muttered the old man, 'not your fault.'

Clancy closed his notebook and stood up. Then he went back out to the verandah and walked around the house.

When he came back he said, 'There are tire tracks out the back—looks like a ute might have been parked out there to carry away the stuff.'

As he sat down again the policeman glanced at Steve

Riley's wrist and said, 'That's an old fashioned watch.'

'Yeah, but it's Swiss,' said Steve, 'keeps excellent time. Belonged to my father. It's an old analogue clockwork thing, but I wouldn't part with it.'

After a moment's quiet thought Clancy walked out to his van and radioed in to Wongalla headquarters, telling them to patrol the roads around the area and to look for a utility, or similar vehicle, that had left Dagworth station not long before.

Then he went back inside and said to Steve Riley, 'Kindly tell us where your mates in the ute are likely to be headed, and whether you've kept any of the stolen money around here.'

How does Clancy know that Steve Riley has been lying and that he was involved in the theft? What one vital clue has give the game away? (Solution at the end of the next yarn.)

Out on the Birdsville Track

The Birdsville police station had a simple procedure that they always followed with tourists and travellers who wanted to drive down the Birdsville Track in the remote, desolate and sometimes dangerous outback.

They insisted that tourists call into the Birdsville police station and lodge their travel plans, so that their destination and expected time of arrival would be known. Then, if they didn't turn up, a search could be started. The police also provided a check list of supplies and equipment the tourists should carry, and gave them a printed page telling them what steps to take in case of a breakdown or other emergency.

Travellers were also given a radio frequency they could use to summon help. They could even (for a small fee) rent a radio transceiver operating on that frequency. The only rule that applied to the use of these small radio sets was that they must be used for legitimate purposes: emergency calls, to report position and progress, or to seek information.

Sadly, some travellers didn't respect the rules. When they discovered there were other tourists on the Birdsville Track at the same time as themselves, also equipped with these small radios, they used them to chat and gossip. They used them as if they were ordinary CB radios.

Police always warned against the abuse of the radio

frequency, and sometimes their warnings were listened to. But sadly, sometimes they were ignored.

The importance of this became clear when one couple broke down and became stranded, just as the wife became ill. They were unable to get through on the special police radio frequency for several hours because a group of tourists further up the track were constantly using that frequency to chat, as if it was a private telephone line.

Eventually the couple did get through and were rescued. But when the offending tourists finally returned their small radio transceivers, they received a stern lecture from a burly police sergeant.

'The use of these radios,' he growled at them, 'is governed by *content*. They are to be used for transmitting and receiving messages of a certain content. The content must be about the weather, or travel conditions, or the need for supplies, or an emergency situation. Any communication outside of the specified range of content is an absolute and utter waste of this powerful and important radio network.'

Moral: Content is what governs the sensible use of powerful communications.

Jesus said: 'Pray then like this: Our Father in heaven . . . ' (Matthew 6:9).

When Jesus taught his first followers how to pray, what he emphasised in the Lord's Prayer was *content*. He focused on what they should pray *about*. He didn't tell them whether they should stand or sit or kneel. He didn't tell them to raise their hands or clasp their hands. He didn't tell them in what language they should pray. He told them what they should pray *about*.

The prayer he provided as a model is brief—so we know prayer doesn't need to be long. It deals with two topic areas: God and us. It puts God first, and begins by asking for God to be glorified. Only secondly does it turn to the needs of human life.

Prayer is a precious gift that is not to be abused by

turning it into a shopping list or a complaint or gossip session. It is to focus on God's glory and then on human need: the content must control every transmission.

Solution to 'The Puzzle of the Midnight Visitor'

As the linen cupboard was windowless, Steve Riley could not have known, from his analogue watch, how long he'd been unconscious—whether the hands were approaching twelve noon or twelve midnight. Indeed, since his uncle was expected at noon the next day, he should have assumed it was noon when he looked at his watch.

What had actually happened was that he had seen the lights of his uncle's car arriving home unexpectedly early and hurried his accomplices out the back door with the loot. He wanted to persuade the policeman that the thieves were long gone and there was no point in searching for them. He failed because Clancy was too sharp for him. As a result his accomplices were caught with the loot, and they implicated Steve in their statements.

The moral from this mystery: The owner may return at any time.

Steve Riley's Uncle Stan came back in exactly the way that Jesus said he will come back: unexpectedly.

Jesus said: 'You don't know when The Boss is coming back! It might be tomorrow, or the day after, or next week, or . . . whenever. So don't slack off. Pass this message on to everyone else, and stay alert' (Mark 12:36–37 AUSSIE BIBLE).

Night Lights

(John 14:1–4)

I am working the night-shift and walking home late,
And the streets are all empty and echo the scrape
Of my shoes as they scuff on the footpath and road;
In the silence I think of the people bestowed
In the comfort of warm beds and snuggled down deep
Who are drifting towards the sweet safety of sleep.

And I pull my coat closer and shiver inside
And I curse my old car and I wish I could ride.
But the garage said two days and now they say three
So I walk in the darkness, a cold refugee.
As I walk I see windows that glow from within
And I faintly hear voices—a soft, friendly din.

I imagine the lives that are lit by those lights
As they huddle around the oil heater tonight.
Are they happy or sad? Do they laugh? Do they cry?
These are things I can't guess. I'm a mere passer-by.
As I trudge in the darkness expecting a storm,
I know one thing: inside, in the light, they are warm!

I pass portraits of happiness, husband and wife,
Each window's a picture of warmness and life.
I remember the warm rooms that I have been in,

And I wish that I wasn't outside but within.
I can hear a night bird give a faint ghostly shriek;
The roadway around me is deserted and bleak.

A dog barks in a yard as I hurry on past,
In the darkness alone I am midnight's outcast.
Each window lights up like a panel of gold
And inside there is coffee and laughter untold;
There is light after light that is gleaming like chrome:
At the heart of the lights is the beat of a home.

There is longing for Home deep in everyone's breast,
And until we all find it we all have no rest.
'In my Father's house now there is many a room.'
So the Bible assures me, and so I assume.
There's a place in our heart for the place we desire,
Where the lights are turned on and the log's on the fire.

The Puzzle of the Killed Counterfeiter

Constable Clancy Paterson was just fetching a cold can of beer from the fridge at the end of a long hot day when the telephone rang.

'Are you the duty police officer at Yallambee?' said the voice at the other end of the line.

'Son, I'm the *only* police office in Yallambee,' replied Clancy. 'What can I do for you?'

'I've just discovered a body—a dead body,' said the voice of the young man on the phone, 'and I wanted to call it in. By the way, I'm a trainee constable. My name's Paul Yates.'

'Well, you tell me where you are, Paul,' said Clancy, 'and I'll be right there.'

Young Paul Yates said that he was at a rail crossing some miles south of the town. Clancy drove out there in the police patrol van and found the young man, standing in the blazing late afternoon sun.

They introduced themselves and shook hands. Then Paul said, 'I'm on holidays from the police academy at Goulburn, and I was driving out to see some relatives of mine on a property out past Wongalla. As I was driving over this rail crossing I spotted something suspicious about a hundred metres up the track. So I pulled over to the side of the road to investigate. When I approached the object I saw it was a man's dead body, so I used my mobile phone to call it in.'

'Thanks for that, young fella,' said Clancy. 'You did the right thing. And you've got a sharp pair of eyes in your head. Now, where's this body?'

Paul led the way down the railway line until they came to a crumpled form beside the track. Clancy knelt down, made sure the man was dead, and then turned him over. His face was badly bruised and his neck was broken. His clothes were dusty and torn, and everything about him suggested that he had come off a passing train and fallen heavily onto the hard, rocky ground beside the tracks.

Suddenly Paul said excitedly, 'I recognise him . . . at least, I think I recognise him.'

Clancy turned to the young man and said, 'Then tell me who he is, son.'

'He's Allan Sullivan,' said Paul.

'And he's a well-known organised crime figure in Sydney,' added Clancy. 'Yeah, even us country coppers know that much. And pretty clearly he came off a passing train. The only train that's run down this track today has been the express from Sydney to Broken Hill, so that must be the train he came off in such a rush. The question is, why?'

'I think I might know the answer,' volunteered the young trainee policeman.

'Very well, Mr Yates,' said Clancy, 'explain what happened and why.'

'Well,' began Paul, 'while I was waiting for you to come I had a bit of a look around, and I discovered that this man's suitcases had come off the train with him. Look up there . . .'

He pointed westwards down the train line, towards the setting sun. 'See, there's a suitcase there. I've already been to have a look at it. And beyond it—a bit further west down the line still—is a second suitcase. It's the second one I think you'll be interested in.'

Constable Paterson followed the eager young man down the track. The first suitcase, with the initials 'A.S.' stamped on it, contained nothing but clothes. But the second case, also stamped 'A.S.', contained something much more interesting. It was packed with money.

Clancy whistled softly as he picked up a bundle of notes and thumbed through them.

'This little lot,' he said, 'must be worth at least $50,000 dollars.'

'But there's more,' interrupted Paul. 'I held these notes up to the sun and there's no watermark on them: they're fakes.'

'Well, that fits in,' Clancy said, 'since Allan Sullivan here—the dead man—has been known to be involved in counterfeiting.'

'Here's how I reconstructed it,' said Paul. 'My guess is that for some reason Allan Sullivan felt under threat on that train—the Sydney to Broken Hill express that you mentioned. Maybe he knew someone was after his counterfeit money. It must have been something like that, because clearly he first threw his suitcases off the train, and then he jumped off himself. But the train was going too fast, and the ground was too rocky, and when he jumped he killed himself. Do you agree, Constable Paterson? That must be what happened, mustn't it?'

Clancy didn't reply for a moment. He stood up and stretched, then collected the two suitcases and began to walk slowly back up the line towards the dead body.

'I hate to puncture your neat theory, young fella,' said Clancy, 'but what you say is impossible. The evidence suggests that what you've described is the impression someone tried to create. What we're looking at here is not only fake money, it's faked evidence. My guess is that what really happened is that Allan Sullivan was murdered on the train, his body thrown off, and then his suitcases thrown off after him—to create the impression that he'd jumped.'

What is it about the evidence that supports Clancy's theory and not Paul's? (Solution at the end of the next yarn.)

Pressing Forward

Dave Rudd was a member of the Snake Gully
Athletics Club. He was a good middle distance
runner, with a chance of qualifying for the state
championships. His trainer was his own father.

Dad Rudd had been a good middle distance runner
himself in his youth, and he worked hard at getting Dave
up to the standard required for the state championships.

It was a Thursday afternoon training session. Dave was
on the track with several other runners, Dad was on the
sidelines with his stop watch at the ready, and the starter
took up his starting pistol.

'Ready,' said the starter. 'On your marks,' and the
runners crouched on their blocks. Then he fired the
starting pistol and they were off.

Dave made a good start and was soon pulling ahead of
the field. As they circled the track he glanced back to see
what the others were doing. Most of the field was well
behind him, but Dave was alarmed to see that his old rival,
Bill Smith, had broken out of the pack, put on a spurt
of speed and started to catch up with him. Dave put his head
down and poured more energy into his pumping legs. But
every few seconds he glanced back to see how close Bill was.

The finish line was now in view and rapidly drawing
closer. Every time Dave glanced back, Bill drew closer and
still closer. At last Bill was almost up with him, stride for
stride. Dave glanced at the finishing line and pushed

harder, then he glanced at Bill, and then glanced again.

They crossed the line almost together.

The judge scratched his chin and looked thoughtful for a moment. After keeping everyone in suspense for what seemed like an age, he finally said, 'I think I'll have to give it to Bill Smith by half a stride.'

Dad Rudd came stalking over to Dave, his face looking black.

'What did you have to go and do that for, Dave?' he thundered.

'Do what, Dad?'

'Give the race away like that!'

'Whaddya mean?'

'You had it won, Dave. You had the whole field, including Bill Smith, beaten—and then you went and gave it all away. It's a good thing today's only practice. If you do that in competition you'll be finished.'

'I don't know what you're talking about, Dad,' complained Dave.

'Don't you just? Well, then, I'll explain. You looked back,' thundered Dad. 'Not once but again and again. You kept on looking back. Every few seconds you were looking back over your shoulder. And every time you looked back you lost distance. That was how you threw the race away.'

'I still don't understand,' said Dave miserably.

'Look, Dave,' explained Dad. 'You can't run forwards—not properly anyway—while you're looking backwards. It just stands to reason. You become less wind efficient, you lose your impetus—everything goes wrong. You can't go forwards looking backwards. You have to learn to ignore the rest of the field and just run your own race. Do that, and you'll do okay.'

Moral: You can't run forwards looking backwards.

The Bible says: 'Forgetting what lies behind and straining forward to what lies ahead, I press on toward the goal for the prize of the upward call of God in Christ Jesus' (Philippians 3:13-14).

There are a few things in this world that can never be changed—and one of them is the past. We can regret the things we've done wrong, the opportunities we've let slip, the mistakes we've made, the wrong directions we've chosen, but regretting them will not change them. The past is sealed, closed, finished and unchangeable. So dwelling on it too much will be destructive in the end: you can't run forwards while looking backwards.

The statement from the Bible above was written by a man named Paul, who before he became a Christian himself had persecuted Christians and hounded them into prison. He may well have been tempted to remember what he'd done and to become bogged down in remorse over his past actions.

But instead he says that he forgets what lies behind and strains forward to what lies ahead.

That's the task that every Christian has. Every Christian is to press on towards the heavenly goal. Christians must not become stuck in the past, for dwelling over-much on yesterday can be like sinking into quicksand. Feel sorrow, ask for forgiveness and move on. The future lies ahead, and there is work to be done as part of reaching the future.

You can't run forwards looking backwards.

Solution to 'The Puzzle of the Killed Counterfeiter'

Clancy's theory is more likely to be correct because the suitcases were found *west* of the body. The train was the Sydney to Broken Hill express, so it must have been travelling west at the time. In other words, the suitcases must have been thrown off the train *after* the body, not before.

The moral from this mystery: The world is full of fakes, but the real remains the real.

The Bible says: 'Cursed is the man who trusts in man and makes flesh his strength, whose heart turns away from the Lord. He is like a shrub in the desert, and shall not see any good come. He shall dwell in the parched places of the wilderness, in an uninhabited salt land. Blessed is the man who trusts in the Lord, whose trust *is* the Lord. He is like a tree planted by water, that sends out its roots by the stream, and does not fear when heat comes' (Jeremiah 17:5-8, emphasis added).

The Ballad of the Good Stockman

(Luke 10:25–37)

Back in 1857,
On a dusty outback road,
A swaggie slowly trudged along,
He had no 'fixed abode'.

He was 'waltzing his Matilda'
From Gunnedah to Gundagai,
Beneath his feet a dusty track,
Above, a clear blue sky.

As he passed beneath a gum tree,
As he came around a bend,
Two bushrangers there attacked him,
Saying: 'You're in trouble, friend.'

They, sailing into the swaggie,
Beat him up and knocked him flat,
They stole his coat and jacket,
They stole his broad-brimmed hat.

They mocked the swaggie laughingly,
Releasing their aggressions.
They took the swag he carried,
They stole his few possessions.

They flung their victim to the road,
They kicked him in the head,
Then mounted up and rode away
And left him there for dead.

An hour later, down the road
Trotted a pony cart,
Bearing the Bishop of Tooralong,
The Very Reverend Mr Smart.

Smart by name and smart by nature,
When he saw the body there
He knew the district wasn't safe
And departed for . . . elsewhere!

The Vicar of Bundiwallop
Was the next to come along.
When he saw the swaggie's body,
Well—his stomach wasn't strong.

He trembled and his face went pale
Then turned a sickly green,
And as the Vicar turned away
He just wished he hadn't seen.

The Vicar of Bundiwallop
Fought a battle in his mind,
Quickly defeating his conscience
And leaving the body behind.

The body lay in the baking sun,
Covered in dust and flies,
Abandoned by the 'nice people',
The 'godly' and the 'wise'.

An Aboriginal stockman
Was riding down that way,
He'd been working on his stock horse
Since before the break of day.

He rode easy in the saddle
Though his working day was long,
And he knew the land he travelled,
Knew its story and its song.

His native name was Pemulwuy:
His employer called him Jacky;
And didn't pay him wages,
Just some flour and 'tobaccy'.

Jacky didn't hesitate
When he thought he saw a corpse,
He took a pull upon the reigns
And climbed down from his horse.

He hurried to the swaggie's side
Then knelt down in the dust,
And muttered softly to himself,
'I think he'll pull through—just.'

He lifted up the swaggie's head,
So beaten, bruised and coshed;
With water from his water bag
The wounds he cleaned and washed.

Some brandy from his hip-flask
He made the swaggie swallow,
And with some more he cleaned the wounds—
The right technique to follow.

Then Jacky got his one clean shirt
Out of his saddle bags;
He ripped it into narrow strips,
Making bandages from rags.

The swaggie's eyelids opened
Though he trembled and he shook.
In a croaking voice he whispered,
'I'm feelin' fairly crook.'

Exhausted by the effort,
He sank back on the sand,
His bandaged head was cradled
In Jacky's strong, black hand.

Then Jacky lifted the swagman
Onto his horse's back:
'I know a place to take ya, boss,
It's not far down the track.'

To get to Harry's Grog Shop,
That was Jacky's plan:
'I think we're gunna make it,
I really think we can.'

They arrived at Lazy Harry's
Later that afternoon,
And by the look of the swaggie
It wasn't a minute too soon.

When Jacky knocked on Harry's door
He received a rude rebuff:
'I don't serve blackfellas here,'
Snarled Harry, 'So you clear off.'

'I've got a bloke needs mending,'
Jacky said, 'He's hurting, boss.'
'Well, if he dies that's one black less,'
Said Harry, 'That's no loss.'

'He's whitefella, not blackfella,
He's one of your mob, boss.'
Still Harry groaned and grumbled,
Said he couldn't give a toss.

Into his pocket Jacky dipped
And pulled out a ten bob note,
He then extracted a second one,
Out of his battered coat.

'I'll pay whatever it costs you, boss,'
Is what the stockman said,
'I'll pay for all his care and grub,
I'll pay for his food and bed.

'And then next week,' said the stockman,
'When I'm back down this way,
If there's any more he's cost you,
The whole of his debt I'll pay.'

The point of the stockman's story
Is impossible to miss,
The point of the story is simply—
That we should behave like this.

The Puzzle of the Flustered Stranger

Constable Clancy Paterson was taking a stroll around the small outback town of Yallambee one quiet, sunny spring morning.

When you're the only policeman in a small town you normally know everyone you meet. That was why Clancy was surprised to see a young man come hurrying around a corner who was a total stranger to him.

The young man appeared not to see Clancy and almost collided with him.

'What's the rush, young fella?' said Clancy as he grabbed the stranger's arm to stop him falling over.

'Sorry . . . sorry . . .' gasped the young man, sounding startled and winded from his near collision with the policeman.

'What's the rush?' repeated Clancy. 'Where's the fire?'

For a moment the young man looked confused and uncertain, then he cleared his throat. 'There's an old lady, back in the cottage just around the corner. She's had a fall. I was just going for a doctor.'

'Come on, show me,' said Clancy as he began striding towards the street corner the young man had indicated. The breathless stranger had no choice but to fall into step beside the tall policeman and try to keep up.

As they walked Clancy said, 'How come I don't know you? Strangers are rare around these parts, and I reckon I know everyone in town.'

'I'm an insurance salesman,' the young man explained. 'I'm new to this part of the state. I'm based over at Wongalla, and this is my first trip to Yallambee. So that's why you haven't seen me before.'

'What's your name?' asked the policeman.

'Ah . . . Brian . . . Brian Johnston.'

As they rounded the corner Brian Johnston pointed to a house two doors away and said, 'That's it. That's where the old lady had a fall.'

'Come and show me,' said Clancy firmly. He ushered the young man before him through the front gate, down the path and up the front steps to the screen door, which was standing half open.

Clancy turned to Brian and said, 'This is Edith Murphy's place.' Then the constable called out through the doorway, 'Edith, are you there? It's me—Constable Paterson.'

'She's had a fall, I tell you,' repeated Brian Johnston. 'She's unconscious.'

'Oh, unconscious, is she?' responded Clancy. 'You hadn't told me that.'

Clancy entered the house, steering Brian Johnston ahead of him. They found Edith lying on the rug in the living room. Her eyes were closed and there was blood streaming from the back of her head. Clancy knelt down and checked her pulse. Even though she was unconscious her breathing was strong and steady. He stepped over to the sideboard, picked up the telephone and called the local GP, Dr Henry Moran. Doc Moran promised to come immediately, and said that he would call for an ambulance from the Wongalla Base Hospital.

Clancy put down the phone and turned back to Brian Johnston. 'Now, exactly what happened here, Mr Johnston?'

The young man swallowed hard and explained.

'I knocked at the front door, and when Mrs Murphy came to the door I told her that I was offering generous deals on property insurance and explained a bit about the sort of deal I could arrange. We stood on the verandah talking for some minutes, and then she said she was interested and left me on the verandah while she went inside to get a copy of her current insurance policy. She was gone for a minute or two and then I heard a crash. Since the door was open, I went straight in to see what had happened, and I found her—just like this—on the floor, unconscious. She must have fallen over and struck her head on a piece of furniture, because her head was bleeding like it is now. And that's when I ran for help. But fortunately, just as I came around the corner I ran into you. I'm so glad I did.'

Brian Johnston took a large white handkerchief out of his pocket and wiped his forehead, which was covered in beads of sweat. Then he sat down heavily in an armchair.

Clancy looked around the room. The furniture was undisturbed except for one drawer in the sideboard that was standing open. Some papers had been pulled out of this drawer and had fallen to the floor. He stooped and picked them up. They were an assortment of forms and legal papers, including Edith Murphy's house and contents insurance policy. Inside the drawer was a small lockable cash box, but this was now open and empty except for a few small coins.

Just then Doc Moran arrived. After greeting Clancy and glancing at the young stranger, he knelt down and examined Edith.

While the doctor was working, Clancy glanced around the room. It was immaculate as always, without a mark or a speck of dust on any of the furniture. Edith was a very careful housekeeper.

After a couple of minutes Doc Moran said, 'There may be a fracture to the skull, and she'll probably have concussion. The ambulance from Wongalla will be here in half an hour or so. In the meantime, I'll clean up her wound and make her comfortable. How did this happen, Clancy?'

'Well, now,' said the policeman slowly, 'that's an

interesting question.' He looked at the young man and said, 'I'll tell you, Mr Brian Johnston—or whatever your real name is—what really happened here.

'You called at the front door, pretending to sell insurance or whatever excuse you use when you intend to get into the homes of old people and steal any cash they have around the place. Edith Murphy is a trusting soul and she invited you in. Somehow you persuaded her to bring out her cash box—perhaps you asked for a small cash deposit. Once she'd unlocked the box you assaulted her and stole the contents. You were fleeing when you ran into me, and had to quickly invent a story on the spot to explain the situation.'

For a moment the young man stuttered and blustered, then he denied everything.

Clancy responded by saying, 'There's no point in denying it, young fella. There are no fewer than five clues that tell me your account of what happened here today is false.'

What are the five clues that show Clancy the young man's story is false? How many of those clues can you find? (Solution at the end of the next yarn.)

The Fable of the Two Fields

Once upon a time, long ago and far away, there was a great and powerful wizard. One summer's afternoon he was driving in his fine carriage, pulled by four white horses, through a beautiful and fertile valley.

This valley was filled with small farms, and as the farmers saw the great and powerful wizard drive past, they would politely raise their caps and bow their heads. Then they would return to their farming. For their lands required much hard work to produce crops each year.

Coming around a bend in the road the wizard's carriage hit a rock. For a moment it tipped over to one side, then it rolled back off the rock and crashed down again. There was an ominous cracking noise and the carriage stopped dead—dragging on the road.

The wizard called to his coachman to stop and got out to take a look at the problem. The front axle had snapped in two. It would need to be replaced.

'Well, your wizardship,' said the coachman, 'can't you just wave your magic wand and make a new axle appear?'

'Under normal circumstances, yes,' replied the wizard. 'But as it happens I've left my magic wand back at the castle, and I'm helpless to fix the axle. Perhaps, coachman, you can do something?'

'I'd love to, your wizardship,' replied the coachman. 'But I belong to the wrong union. Only the WWU (the

Wood Workers' Union) can repair an axle of that sort. I belong to the CDU (the Coach Drivers' Union), and I'd be in all sorts of bother if I tried to do a job that belongs to a brother from another union. There'd be a demarcation dispute, and we wouldn't want that now, would we?'

'No, of course not,' muttered the wizard, puzzled as to how he could get out of his fix.

Just then one of the local farmers, young Farmer Giles, approached and said, 'Look, I'm not a member of any union, and I'm pretty handy at fixing things. Perhaps I can help.'

And he did. He cut down a small tree, trimmed it to size and used it to replace the broken axle. He worked at this for two hours in the blazing summer sun, but none of the other farmers in the valley (all of whom could see what was happening) bothered to come and help.

When he had finished Farmer Giles waved the wizard on his way and went back to work on his farm, thinking no more about it.

But a week later the wizard returned, late at night, and knocked on Farmer Giles' door. 'I have a gift for you,' explained the wizard, 'to thank you for repairing my carriage.' He led Farmer Giles outside and waved his magic wand over one of Giles' fields.

'This field,' said the wizard, 'is now unlike any other field in the valley. This field, and this field alone, can grow grain that will make you fit and healthy, and will stop you growing any older. It may not taste as nice as the grain from other fields, but it will do you much more good.'

The wizard's words proved to be absolutely true. Grain from the special field never did taste quite as nice as grain from other fields, but when Farmer Giles and his family ate the grain from that magic field they were fit and strong, their colds and flu went away, and they stopped aging.

So each planting season Farmer Giles had a dilemma as he looked at his limited supply of seed. Would he plant his seed in a normal field that would grow nice-tasting grain? Or would he plant it in the special field that would produce grain that would not be as nice on the tongue, but would do much more good in the long run?

Moral: Choices are often between the short-term and the long-term—between the temporary and the permanent.

The Bible says: 'For the one who sows to his own flesh will from the flesh reap corruption, but the one who sows to the Spirit will from the Spirit reap eternal life' (Galatians 6:8).

Solution to 'The Puzzle of the Flustered Stranger'

Here are the five clues that Clancy spotted:

1. The telephone was on the sideboard right beside the body. If the young man had been telling the truth he would have used the phone to ring for help—not run out onto the streets of a town in which he was a stranger, where he couldn't know where to find a doctor or medical help. The obvious presence of the telephone right beside the body showed the young man to be a liar.

2. The cash box was empty except for a few small coins. No one would keep a lockable cash box and put nothing in it except a few small coins. Therefore most of the money, all the folding money, was missing.

3. In the young man's story he claimed that Edith Murphy had kept him waiting on the front verandah, but in small country towns people—even visiting insurance salesmen—are always invited inside.

4. On colliding with the policeman the young man became more distressed, not less. Since Edith was a stranger to him, her injuries could not explain his distress—unless he had inflicted

them himself, and the presence of the policeman made him fear that his guilt would be discovered. Given the story he told, his level of continuing distress gave away his guilt.

5. The room was immaculate without a mark or a speck of dust anywhere. If Edith had hit her head on a piece of furniture as she fell, there would have been blood on an edge or a corner of one of the pieces of furniture. But there wasn't.

The moral from this mystery: 'Be sure your sin will find you out' (Numbers 32:23).

Dr Pym's Academy

(Matthew 21:28–32)

There was a Dr Percy Pym
(Quite possibly you've heard of him)
Who ran a modest school for boys,
Marked by lessons full of noise.

'Standforth!' Dr Pym would shout,
'Go and sweep the bike shed out!'
'No, sir,' said Standforth sullenly,
'Sweeping out is not for me.'

'Bottomly!' then Pym would boom,
'To the bike shed—with a broom!'
'Yes, sir, to the bike shed—right away.
I'll do anything you say.'

But for Bottomly it was ruse—
He just wanted an excuse
To escape from history class
And kick a football in the grass.

Standforth, on the other hand,
Was feeling somewhat less than grand.
And, despite the words he said,
He swept out the school bike shed.

Now, which one was the honest lad?
Which one made his teacher glad?
The one who said but didn't do?
Or the one who finally came through?

God's attitude is much the same:
Empty words are full of shame.
Heaven is reserved for those
Who do more than merely strike a pose!

The Puzzle of the Downpour of Death

When it rained in the small outback township of Yallambee, it really rained. For three days the rain had poured down in buckets. The unsealed roads leading to the properties around the township had turned into quagmires of mud. Wallaby Creek—the creek that circled around the township on three sides—was normally a small trickle at the bottom of a gully, but after days of heavy rain it was running a banker.

Constable Clancy Paterson was sitting in the office that was the front room of the police cottage, catching up on his paperwork and thankful that he didn't have to go back out into the downpour.

As he finished filling in one form and turned to the next he glanced up and saw a battered old ute slide to a stop in a spray of mud. The driver, wearing a Drizabone coat and an Akubra pulled down low, leaped out and ran up the front path. A moment later there was a heavy pounding on the front door.

Clancy flung open the door to see a dripping wet Alf Schooler standing on his front verandah.

'Come in, Alf,' said the policeman, 'and get those wet things off.'

'No, no—we need your help, Clancy,' replied the visitor in an agitated tone. 'We need you to drive us back out to my place. The creek's up over the road. I managed to make it into town, but my ute'll never make it back again.

We need you to run us out in your four-wheel-drive.'

'Who's "we"?' asked Clancy.

'Doc Moran and me,' Alf responded breathlessly. 'It's me wife, Val. She's had a fall. We've gotta get the doc out to her.'

Clancy grabbed his own Drizabone off the hall stand, slapped his blue police Akubra on his head, called out to his young wife Matty that he had to go out, and followed Alf into the rain.

'Where's the doc now?' asked Clancy.

'Waiting in the ute,' replied the anxious farmer.

'You go and join him,' instructed the policeman. 'I'll get the patrol van out of the shed and drive around the front.'

A few minutes later the white Nissan Patrol with a blue police stripe down each side came to halt beside Alf Schooler's ute. The two men in the front seat of the ute jumped out, ran through the rain and climbed into the back seat of the Patrol.

Old Doc Moran was puffing with the exertion as he said, 'Thanks for this, Clancy. My Holden wouldn't make it if the creek's up over the road, and Alf's ute is about to give up the ghost.'

Once they left the sealed roads of the little township, Clancy engaged the four-wheel-drive and slowed down. The Patrol bounced, splashed and slid its way over the muddy, rutted gravel road.

About ten kilometres out of town they came to the point where the creek crossed the road. The bitumen disappeared beneath a swirling current of brown water. Clancy dropped down to the lowest gear and slowly eased the vehicle through the torrent. They could feel the floodwaters tugging at the van as the Patrol struggled to keep a grip. The worst moment came when a heavy branch from a gum tree, swept along by the stream, thumped into the vehicle. The Patrol swung sideways, but Clancy got it under control again. A moment later they were climbing up the far side of the gully.

The policeman pushed the van along as fast as he thought it safe to go. 'Just exactly what did you say happened to Val?' he asked Alf.

'Val hasn't been all that well for a few days,' the farmer replied. 'Losing her balance, like, and not steady on her feet. She had a fall in the shed this morning that left cuts and bruises over her face.'

Doc Moran interrupted irritably. 'You should have brought her in, Alf. You don't ignore symptoms like that.'

'Yeah, sure, doc. But you know Val. Didn't want to come.'

'Carry on, Alf,' said the constable. 'What happened then?'

'Well, Val was walking down the hall when she seemed to lose her balance and trip and fall. She came down hard on the hall dresser. Hit her head on the edge of it. Knocked unconscious she was. I couldn't bring her round. And the telephone's out—washed away, I guess—so I made her as comfortable as possible and came into town to get the doc.'

Just then they reached the Schooler property. They turned off the road and drove up through the paddocks, Alf leaping in and out of the Patrol to open and close each gate. Finally they were in the home yard, with Alf's blue cattle dog standing on the verandah, barking furiously at them.

The three men hurried into the house. As the rain drummed down on the corrugated iron roof, Doc Moran knelt down beside Val Schooler, who lay in the hall with a pillow under her head and a blanket over her. Her eyes were closed and her face pale.

After just a few seconds the doctor looked up and said, 'I'm sorry, Alf. She's gone.'

Alf swallowed hard, blinked rapidly, then walked over to the window. He stood there with his back towards the doctor and the police constable, staring blindly out at the rain, his hands trembling.

After a minute or so he turned around, walked a few steps and collapsed heavily into an armchair.

Doc Moran was still kneeling over the body examining the injuries. Glancing over his shoulder at the farmer, he said, 'Clancy, I'd prescribe a hot cup of tea for Alf, preferably with a shot of brandy in it. Can you see to that?'

Clancy nodded and walked out to the kitchen.

When he came back he was carrying a steaming hot mug of tea.

'I even managed to find the brandy,' he said. 'Come on, Alf, drink this. It'll do you the world of good.'

The farmer accepted the mug of tea with trembling hands and began to sip it.

Doc Moran pulled the blanket up over Val Schooler's face and stood up.

'What killed her?' asked the policeman.

'Oh, there's no doubt about that. It was this blow here,' replied the medical man, kneeling down again, pulling back the blanket and pointing to a deep wound in the dead woman's forehead. 'A sharp downward blow on the top of her forehead—that's what did it.'

As he pulled the blanket back into place and straightened up, Clancy stood in thoughtful silence. Then he turned to the doctor and said, 'Does that mean what I think it means?'

'I'm afraid so,' the doctor replied.

Clancy walked over and sat down beside Alf, who was still sipping his tea and staring down at the floor.

'Now, Alf,' said Clancy firmly. 'Do you want to tell me what *really* happened?'

What did really happen? How does Clancy know that the story Alf Schooler told was false? What vital clue has revealed the truth? (Solution at the end of the next yarn.)

The Fable of the Very Special Bus

Jenny had grown up in a fairly normal, reasonably happy middle-class family. She had gone through school and got herself a job.

But all through her young life, Jenny had been aware of the buses.

They were special buses. Oh, there were plenty of perfectly normal buses around the place—buses that would take you into town, to the shops or wherever. But in addition there were these other buses. They were specials. Not in the usual sense that buses sometimes have the word 'special' on their front indicator boards. No, these special buses were very special.

And they stopped at special bus stops. On every one of these bus stops were the words 'Signal Driver'. Jenny had seen the very special buses from time to time—either stopping at one of the special bus stops to pick up a passenger, or picking up someone on a street corner or even in the middle of the road if that person had waved the bus down.

The story that people in the city and suburbs told about these buses was that they were 'paradise specials'. They would take you to paradise—the celestial city—and were provided by the Great King of the celestial city at a terrible price to himself (a price so terrible people spoke about it only in whispers).

Some folk mocked these ideas. There was, they said, no

celestial city, no paradise, to be carted off to. And even if by some chance there was, these buses were just buses and there was no guarantee they would take you there.

Jenny had listened to what people said and had seen the buses, and she had even caught a glimpse of the bus driver's face: a terrible yet wonderful face. She was fairly confident that the buses *were* as special as their indicator boards said they were. She was fairly certain that these special buses *would* take anyone who got on board to the place listed on the front of the bus—the celestial city.

But even though this is what she thought, Jenny never signalled the driver, never asked one of these special buses to stop, and never got on board.

There was so much else going on in her life that somehow she never got around to it. There was study to do and exams to pass. Then there were job interviews, and a career to begin. There were boyfriends, and then that very special boyfriend, and marriage, and a home to buy, and children being born. Life moved along so swiftly that Jenny never found time to 'signal the driver'.

As the days, weeks, months and years of her life ticked by, Jenny would often pass one of the special bus stops. She might stand for a while and read the offer of a free trip on the paradise line. She might study the timetable. But then she would think of all she had to do and she would walk quickly on—before the bus came.

She was once walking down a cold, windy street late at night when things in her life were not going well. She came across a special bus stop and sat on the seat there. At that moment she thought: 'I feel so miserable, I'm just going to sit here until the paradise bus comes, and I will signal the driver, and I will get on board. It's time I did. My life in this world is so unhappy, I have no alternative.'

But somehow she didn't wait. Still feeling miserable, she got up and wandered away before the bus arrived. All the habits of a lifetime conspired to keep her restless, unable to sit still long enough to wait for the special bus.

On another occasion, on a windy autumn afternoon, she saw one of her oldest friends, an old school friend, at the end of the street. She was about to call out and wave when she saw that this friend was looking in the opposite direction, was waving down a paradise bus that had just come around the corner, and was getting on board. Jenny felt annoyed by this—although she couldn't have told you why. She felt she had been deserted by her old friend. She angrily snatched up her shopping bag and firmly told herself that she'd never be silly enough to signal the driver and get on board one of *those* buses.

But at the same time, she knew that she should.

It would mean the end of all the plans she had for her life. It would mean that she was no longer steering her own path—the driver of the special bus (the terrible, wonderful driver) would take over steering her life where *he* wanted her to go. But she still knew that she should— that she should fight it no longer, that she should give in, go to the bus stop, wait for the bus and 'Signal Driver'.

Will she ever do it? Or will she still be waiting when death comes to take her in entirely the other direction? How will Jenny's story end?

Many people are like Jenny. They hear the good news of new life and a fresh start that God offers. They hear the invitation to turn from their way to his way—the invitation to ask Jesus to forgive them, to change them and to take over the running of their life both now and forever.

But they never quite get around to doing it. They never raise their hand to signal the driver. They never say to God: 'Me too. Please, Jesus, take me with you to paradise.'

The Bible says: 'Everyone who calls on the name of the Lord will be saved' (Romans 10:13).

Solution to 'The Puzzle of the Downpour of Death'

Seeing Alf reluctant to speak, Clancy said, 'Do you want me to say it? Would that be easier?'

Alf nodded.

'Well, I know you two always argued a lot. Everyone in town knew that. Real shouting matches they were. This time it came to blows, didn't it?'

Alf nodded again.

Clancy continued, 'That's why she's got those cuts and bruises on her face. It had nothing to do with falling over in the shed, did it? And then it got worse. Somehow the row got worse. I guess you lost your temper and hit her with something. She didn't fall and trip, did she? She's lying there now because you hit her. That's the truth, isn't it, Alf?'

The farmer nodded.

'You see,' explained Clancy, 'Doc Moran can tell that Val was killed by "a sharp downward blow on the top of her forehead". If she'd really fallen against the hall dresser it would have been an upward blow, a blow coming up into the forehead from below. But it wasn't. It was a "downward blow on the top of her forehead". That can only mean she was struck from above—say, by someone with their arm raised above her head, striking down at her. Is that how it happened, Alf?'

Again, the farmer nodded.

The moral from this mystery: Habits are first cobwebs, then cables.

Violent arguments between husband and wife are not part of God's plan for marriage. And yet they were part of Alf and Val's marriage. And once bad habits begin, they continue. Jesus said, 'I tell you for certain that anyone who sins is a slave of sin!' (John 8:34 CEV).

The Biggest Barbecue in Bourke

(Luke 14:15–24)

Out in the outback town of Bourke,
The mayor was a fella named Darby.
And on the banks of the Darling River
He decided to throw a party.

He got in some carcasses of beef,
Soft drinks and barrels of beer,
Then wrote out the invitations
As the big day drew near.

All the ideas, planning and preparation
Involved a great deal of work.
The wording found on each invitation
Was: 'The Biggest Barbie in Bourke.'

An enormous barbecue was planned
By the mayor, Mr William Darby.
He paid for food and the drink himself,
As the host of the great big barbie.

Slowly the invitations came back,
And each one had an excuse:
A 'no' was all that Darby got back
From each Kenneth and Wendy and Bruce.

'I'm sorry, old mate,' one of them wrote,
'I've got to check up on some land.'
'I'm sorry,' another one of them said,
'There's something else I've got planned.'

'I've bought a new bullock,' one of them moaned,
'And the beast is acting all queer.
So I can't come out when the beast is like this,
I think I'd better stay here.'

The bloke who took all these phone calls
Told Darby just what they had said.
And Darby was not at all happy,
In fact, he began to see red.

Mr William Darby gave orders:
'Round up whoever you can,
Invite the poor and the old and the sick,
Any child or woman or man.'

So they started to come as the barbie began,
Those who really needed a meal.
Still Darby insisted, 'Go and get more,
We've got plenty of beer, beef and veal.

'Keep going, don't stop, go further afield,
Search the back roads and rough gravel track.
Find the swaggies and shearers and tramps and the like,
And bring every one of them back.

'As for the others, the ones who said "no",
Those names that made up the list,
If they turn up now, then don't let them in.
Those ingrates will never be missed.'

The Puzzle of Devil's Gap

The road between the small outback town of Yallambee and the larger regional centre of Wongalla ran through a gap in the hills that gave their name to one of the oldest properties in the district: Blue Hills.

At one point this road through the hills was known locally as 'Devil's Gap' because the road there was narrow, with a steep cliff climbing on one side and a steep fall away into the valley on the other.

When Constable Clancy Paterson received a phone call telling him there had been a road accident in Devil's Gap he feared the worst. The caller was the driver of the car concerned, ringing on his mobile phone.

'Has anyone been injured?' asked Clancy.

There was a long silence before the caller finally replied, 'Yes.'

Clancy said he'd be out there immediately. He called out to his wife to phone the district ambulance headquarters in Wongalla and have them dispatch an ambulance to the scene. Then the constable hurried out to the police patrol van and roared off up the Wongalla road in the direction of Devil's Gap.

It was a clear sunny morning, but it had been raining earlier and in places the road was wet and dangerous. The shoulders and ditches on the roadsides were all still thick with mud—the sun not having yet dried them out.

Some distance out of town Clancy's patrol van started climbing into the hills. A few minutes later, rounding a bend, he came upon the scene of the accident. A car was wedged against a tree next to a section of smashed guard railing, dangling dangerously over the valley below.

Clancy parked the patrol van and hurried over to the smashed vehicle. Sitting in the driver's seat was a dazed looking young man wearing a formal dinner suit.

'Come on, son, out of there,' said Clancy gruffly. 'This vehicle is too close to the edge for my liking. Slide over here and climb out this side. You can sit in the patrol van and tell me your story.'

The young man, who appeared to be in his mid-twenties, did as he was told.

'Are you the one who called in the accident?' asked Clancy.

The young man nodded.

'You said someone had been injured—where are they?'

By way of response the young man walked over to the smashed guardrail at the side of the road and pointed to the valley below. Several hundred metres below them, sprawled on an outcrop of rocks, was the twisted body of a young woman dressed in a formal ball gown.

Finally the young man spoke. 'Do you think she'd dead?'

'Almost certainly, son,' said Clancy gently, 'but I have to check just in case.'

From the boot of the police patrol van he fetched a length of rope and tied one end of it to a guard post that hadn't been knocked out of place. Using the rope to steady himself, the policeman clambered down the steep slope. As soon as he got close to the body he could see the young woman was dead. Her body was twisted at an awkward angle, her face was white, there was blood on the rock, and there was no sign of life or movement. Still, Clancy finished his task by checking for a pulse or breath. There was none.

He climbed back up the slope again, going hand over hand up the rope to reach the top. As he did so the ambulance arrived. He told them the accident victim was dead, and then went to talk to the young man.

Taking out a notebook Clancy said, 'You up to answering a few questions?'

The young man nodded.

'Name?'

'Todd Morton. That's my girlfriend, Linda Quigley, down there on the rocks.'

Clancy jotted the names down in his notebook and then said, 'Okay, tell me what happened.'

'We were driving back from the B and S ball—the Bachelors and Spinsters Ball—at Wongalla last night . . .'

Glancing at the young man's immaculate and spotless dinner suit Clancy interrupted to ask, 'You were there all night?'

The young man nodded and then continued. 'The road was wet and the roadsides were all muddy so I was being careful. But just as we were passing through Devil's Gap a truck came around the bend at us, a cattle truck. It was way over the white line—half on our side of the road. I tried to break and swerve to avoid it without going over the edge, but I lost control—smashed into the guard railing, almost went straight over the edge, and then hit the tree.'

'How did your girlfriend end up down there?' asked the policeman, pointing to the valley floor.

'She was unconscious after the accident,' said the young man. 'Because the car was sort of teetering on the edge I didn't think it was safe to leave her in the passenger's seat, so I lifted her out and was carrying her to safety when I slipped in the mud at the roadside. I slid down onto my knees, lost my grip on Linda and she went over the side.'

At this point he started to weep as he explained that he hadn't meant to let her go, that she just slipped out of his arms when he lost his balance and slid down in the mud.

When he'd recovered, Clancy asked, 'What about the truck that forced you off the road?'

'It didn't stop,' replied the young man. 'It was going so fast I doubt the driver even saw what happened to us.'

Clancy left the young man sitting in the patrol van, walked over to the edge of the road and looked down into the valley. The ambulance officers were in the process of recovering the young woman's body. Seeing what was happening seemed to make up Clancy's mind for him.

He walked back to the police vehicle and said to the young man, 'I'll have to continue questioning you back at the police station. I should warn you that you may wish to have your solicitor present—the charge is likely to be murder.'

Why does Clancy believe that the young man has murdered his girlfriend? What one vital piece of evidence shows that his story is untrue? (Solution at the end of the next yarn.)

The Fable of the Really Useful Jug

Once upon a time, a wise old wizard set up a holiday home for himself (well away from the castle, where the king expected him to work all the time). This holiday cottage was deep inside a dark and mysterious wood.

Once the cottage had been built the wizard set about making all the cooking and eating utensils he might need. He got out his potter's wheel, and, using only the very finest clay, turned pots and jugs and plates and cups and every type of crockery item he might need or you could imagine. Then he placed these pieces in the kiln and fired them until they were perfect.

Once his crockery set was complete, the wizard (being a wizard) tapped each item with his wand and brought it to life. He wanted crockery that would wash itself up after dinner and pack itself away in the cupboard.

But over time the pieces of living crockery—with their little arms and legs and faces—all developed quite distinct personalities. Some were keen to help, eager to leap into the hot soapy water in the sink and wash themselves up after dinner. But others seemed not to mind being grimy and covered in streaks of fat, and would sit around for a day or more before they bothered to have a bath and put themselves away.

There was one particular jug who was known to the others as Toby. This Toby Jug was not the least interested in being of use to his wizard master. He was a curious jug who wanted to explore the world, to play and have fun.

Toby Jug liked nothing more than running outside on a rainy day and rolling in the mud. He made friends with the chickens that lived in the hen house behind the cottage and the pigs that lived in the pig pen at the bottom of the yard. When he had spent the day with these friends, he often came home to the cottage covered in smelly muck.

All the other plates and cups and saucers and jugs and pots complained that he was on the nose and very offensive to be near. But Toby Jug just ignored them, and no matter how dirty he was he would sometimes sit around for days before he bothered with a hot bath and a clean up.

All of this, of course, was noticed by the wizard, who said: 'Well, look at you, Toby Jug. I can hardly use you for storing fresh cream or milk. I can't put a pint of the best beer into you, can I, Toby? So I'll have to find another use for you. And I have no choice—I shall have to use you for all the dirty jobs. When I clean out the grease trap under the sink, you can sit there to catch the waste. And when some food in the fridge has gone off and is smelling horrible, I'll scrape it into you to take outside and throw it in the garbage. I might even put you under my bed as a chamber pot. Those are the only sorts of jobs you are fit for, Toby Jug.'

This news alarmed Toby Jug enormously, and from that day on he was a changed jug. He washed himself up every night and kept himself clean every day—and before long he was back at his old work of holding fresh cream or milk.

Moral: Horses pick the courses they want to run on.

'Therefore, if anyone cleanses himself from what is dishonourable, he will be a vessel for honourable use, set apart as holy, useful to the master of the house, ready for every good work' (2 Timothy 2:21).

Here is a challenge: try to come up with a list of three ways you could be useful to God tomorrow.

Solution to 'The Puzzle of Devil's Gap'

The key to exposing young Todd Morton's story as a lie was his spotless formal dinner suit. If, as he claimed, he had fallen in the mud of the roadside while carrying his unconscious girlfriend, then the suit would be splattered with mud. It wasn't—so he wasn't telling the truth.

The moral from this mystery: There any many ways of running off the road in our journey through life, but only one way of getting through safely.

Jesus said: 'I am the way, and the truth, and the life. No one comes to the Father except through me' (John 14:6).

Fair Dinkum with God

(Luke 18:9–14)

Two blokes wandered into a church
In the midst of a country town.
The day was the hot, the church was cool,
The sun was blazing down.

The church was old and built of stone,
It was cool in the summer heat.
The doors stood open invitingly,
Welcoming weary feet.

Alan Gently was a cattleman
And a Shire Council member,
Wearing his new imported suit
Even in a hot December.

Sam Hunt was a used car dealer,
He was known as 'Slippery Sam',
He'd always put one over you
With a dodgy sort of scam.

Both sat down in the cool and the shade
And both began to think.
While Gently's pride was swelling,
Sam's heart began to shrink.

The thoughts in Alan Gently's head
Were all about his qualities,
About his upright 'niceness'
And lack of foolish frivolities.

But Slippery Sam began to feel
A creeping sort of shame.
He thought of the dodgy deals he'd done
And the people he'd caused some pain.

'Dear God,' thought Alan Gently,
'I'm glad I'm as nice as I am,
Religious and well respected,
And not like Slippery Sam.'

A tear trickled down the cheek
Of wicked old Slippery Sam.
'Forgive me, God,' is what he thought,
'I'm not a nice sort of man.'

And as those two walked back outside
To the heat that boiled and fried,
Slippery Sam, in the eyes of God,
Was the one who was justified.

To those whom God finds humble
And fair dinkum, he'll give a place,
While those who have their nose in the air
Are sure to fall flat on their face.

The Puzzle of the Bothersome Brother

Constable Clancy Paterson and his wife Matty had been invited to a dinner party. Old Bert Dawson and his wife Dotty had asked them to dinner at their property on the Wongalla Road: Jindawarrabell Station.

In consequence Clancy was—rarely for him—not wearing his police uniform. Even more rarely for him, he was wearing a suit and tie.

'Do I really have to get dressed up like this?' he complained for the twentieth time.

'Yes, you do,' said Matty, repeating the reply she had been giving ever since they had started dressing for dinner.

'But you know how much I hate wearing ties, Matty love,' complained Clancy.

'Bert and Dotty's guest is that big lawyer from Sydney, that Geoffrey Hughes man. He's one of the most high-powered lawyers in the country. His name is often in the newspapers. So the Dawsons are trying to show him that we country folk can be just as posh as his city friends by turning on a proper dinner party. And that means proper clothes, and that means you, Clancy. So stop complaining and get on with tying your tie.'

Clancy did stop complaining, but he didn't stop muttering under his breath as he struggled with a windsor knot. Finally he and Matty were dressed, and Matty found a clothes brush to brush down Clancy's suit coat (while he told her not to fuss). They got into the police patrol van and drove out to Jindawarrabell Station.

At about the point where they went off the bitumen onto the gravel, Clancy said, 'How come Bert Dawson knows someone as important as this Geoffrey Hughes anyhow?'

'Dotty was explaining to me,' replied Matty. 'When Bert led the farmers' group in that law case over water rights against the state government, Geoffrey Hughes was the lawyer they hired to prepare their case for the Supreme Court.'

'Ah, I see,' muttered Clancy. Then, after a few more minutes of silence, he asked, 'And how come such a high-powered lawyer is visiting Jindawarrabell?'

'Dotty told me that too,' answered Matty. 'It seems that Geoffrey Hughes has always wanted to see a real sheep station at work, so after they won their court case, Bert invited Mr Hughes to have a holiday at Jindawarrabell.'

'But the court case was last year some time.'

'I know. Apparently it's taken Mr Hughes all this time to find a spare week in his diary when he could take a break.'

On the whole the dinner party was a success. A number of Yallambee's leading citizens were there: the shire president, the bank manager, the Anglican minister, the headmaster of the school and so on.

After the main course, while the dessert was being served, several of the guests began boasting to the visiting lawyer about their clever local policeman, Clancy Paterson.

Clancy went quite pink with embarrassment as people around the dinner table recounted his success at solving various crimes and puzzles. They talked about the case of the counterfeiter thrown off a train; the time Clancy happened to be on the spot to solve the circus robbery at the nearby town of Wongalla; the way he'd exposed a fake salesman trying to fleece one of the town's elderly citizens; the way he'd uncovered an attempted fraud involving an Arthur Streeton painting—and so on.

After this recital Geoffrey Hughes said, 'Well, Constable Paterson, let me have a go at challenging you with a puzzle of my own. I'll tell you a story—a true story—about something that happened to me as a young lawyer, and I'll tell it in such a way as to set you a puzzle. Then let's see if you can solve the mystery.'

Clancy looked uncomfortable, but everyone else at the table encouraged Geoffrey Hughes to continue.

'Well, it was like this,' said Hughes. 'There was a man named Charlie Smith. He was born in Sydney but he ran away from home when he was just fourteen years old. Why I don't know—I never found out—but he did. Anyway, he had no contact with his family for the rest of his long life.

'For most of that life he travelled around the outback doing a variety of jobs. But in late middle age he settled in Lightning Ridge, and a few years later, as luck would have it, he struck a rich vein of opal. He ended up a very wealthy man. He never married. He just had a local woman come in three days a week to do his housekeeping for him. He lived very simply, and kept his money in the local bank.

'As he was dying in the local hospital he gave an envelope—an old, yellowed, envelope—to the nurse on duty and asked her to give it to his brother Jack. She showed the envelope to the doctor who looked inside and found a hand-written note leaving all of Charlie's considerable property to this brother Jack. So the doctor took it to the local bank manager, whose bank looked after Charlie's account, and the bank manager passed it on to his head office, and the head office of the bank came to my law firm to find this missing brother—Jack Smith.

'We had no information about the man except his name and a yellowed old photograph of the two brothers standing side by side as young boys. It had been taken nearly sixty years earlier. We knew it was a photo of the two brothers because Charlie had written on the back 'Me and Jack at the age of ten'. But that photo and the man's name was all we had to go on—and my job was to find this brother and pass on his inheritance to him. And I didn't have much information about Charlie Smith himself either—just a clipping from the local newspaper showing him with a large opal, taken a year or so before his death, and deeds to his mining claim and so on.

'Now, the name Jack Smith is not that uncommon—so the name didn't help very much. But I put an ad in *The Sydney Morning Herald* calling on Jack Smith, brother of the late Charlie Smith, to come forward. Well, about a hundred blokes did come forward. Nevertheless I was able to pick the real Jack Smith—the real brother—out of that crowd immediately. How did I do it?'

Having told his story, Geoffrey Hughes sat back in his chair with a satisfied grin. Everyone else around the table looked puzzled: how had the lawyer been able to pick out the missing brother from that crowd of a hundred or so applicants?

However, Clancy didn't look baffled at all. 'Now that's not fair, Mr Hughes,' he said. 'You've asked me an easy one. You should have made it harder.'

'If you think it's so easy, Mr Paterson,' said Geoffrey Hughes, 'tell me the solution. How was I able to pick out the brother from those hundred or so applicants?'

Yes, how was he able to? Clancy knows the answer—do you? (Solution at the end of the next yarn.)

Jungle Doctor's Vaccine

The Jungle Doctor looked up from the microscope that he had been crouched over in the small laboratory of the jungle hospital in East Africa.

Turning to his assistant with a smile of triumph on his face, he said, 'I believe we've finally done it. This new vaccine seems to be doing the job of fighting off the enteric fever virus.'

'Good news, bwana,' said the Jungle Doctor's assistant. 'Now we need to make sufficient quantities to inoculate all the people in the district.'

'Quite right,' said the doctor, 'and here's what we'll do . . .'

He explained his plans carefully. Over the next twelve hours a kind of miniature manufacturing plant was set up in the glassware on the laboratory bench, and soon the vaccine was being produced in sufficient quantities to begin distribution.

At this point the Jungle Doctor called a meeting of all his local assistants—all the dressers and male nurses. They had to meet on the verandah of the hospital as there was no room in the small building large enough to hold them all.

Holding up a small bottle of clear liquid, the Jungle Doctor said, 'Now, men, this is the vaccine we've been hoping for. Bottles of this vaccine are being produced in our small laboratory quite quickly now—so your task is to take this vaccine and inoculate everyone in the surrounding villages.'

The men gathered around nodding their dark heads, their eyes glued to his face as he continued his explanation.

'The enteric fever which has done so much damage in neighbouring districts is now invading our part of the country. With this vaccine we're ready to fight it. But I can't do this job alone. It is up to you. It will need many pairs of feet going to many small villages throughout the district. You must take vaccine and needles and inject the vaccine into every inhabitant of every village.'

'But, bwana,' said one of the men, a worried expression on his face, 'what if they refuse the vaccine? What shall we do then?'

'Then you must accept their decision. But you must try to persuade them,' replied the Jungle Doctor. 'Tell them about the terrible disease that is coming, and tell them of the power of this medicine to protect them against that disease—just as a shield will protect against a spear thrown by an enemy.'

'But, bwana,' said the same man, who had always been a bit of a troublemaker, 'can we do this? Do we have the authority to inject everyone with this new medicine?'

'I have,' said the Jungle Doctor firmly, and out of his pocket he pulled a letter and held it up. The letter was written on official letterhead, and at the bottom was the signature of no less a person than the president of the entire nation. The letter gave the doctor, and the staff of his jungle hospital, full authority to vaccinate everyone in their district.

'The president himself,' explained the Jungle Doctor, 'has give full authority to me, and I am telling you to act on my authority. Go to every village, speak to every person, pass on the important news, warn them of the danger, tell them of this medicine that will protect them against that danger, and vaccinate everyone who agrees to be vaccinated.'

Moral: Good news must be shared.

Jesus said something very similar to his first followers, just before he left them. 'All authority in heaven and on earth has been given to me. Go therefore and make disciples of all nations . . . And behold, I am with you always, to the end of the age' (Matthew 28:18–20).

Solution to 'The Puzzle of the Bothersome Brother'

Charlie and Jack Smith were identical twins. Geoffrey Hughes knew that they were twins because on the back of the photograph of them as small boys were the words 'Me and Jack at the age of ten'. In other words, they were the same age, and therefore twins. He had seen the recent newspaper photograph of Charlie Smith so he knew what he looked like as an adult. He picked out from the crowd of applicants the one man who looked identical: and, sure enough, that was the brother.

The moral from this mystery: 'Pick the difference between the twins.'

Charlie and Jack Smith were identical twins—identical, that is, in all but one vital factor: one was alive and one was dead.

The world is like that. We are all identical—not in appearance but in our essential humanity—except for this one vital difference: some are dead and some are alive.

Some people in the world, who appear on the surface to be just like everyone else, are spiritually dead. Others are spiritually alive. No matter how much they are alike in every other aspect of their humanity, this is the big division.

Jesus calls these two groups the 'sheep' and the 'goats'. The sheep (the spiritually alive) have turned from their way to God's way, have been forgiven and re-connected to God. The goats (the spiritually dead) have no living contact with the Living God.

Jesus said that although we can't tell the difference between the spiritually alive and the spiritually dead, he can. And when he returns in judgment 'he will separate them as a shepherd separates the sheep from the goats' (Matthew 25:32 NLT). The difference between eternal life and eternal destruction is the difference between the sheep and the goats.

Which are you? Sheep? Or goat?

The Ballad of the Farm Workers

(Matthew 20:1–16)

Back in the Great Depression
When work was hard to find,
There was one man—a farmer—
Who was unusually kind.

Wheat harvesting was over,
It was time for baling hay,
And the farmer needed workers—
He would need some all that day.

He drove into the township
To the Ettamogah Pub,
And there he told loungers:
'Ten shillings plus your grub.

'That's the pay I'm offering
If you work for me today.
Are there any takers
For this work of baling hay?'

A dozen blokes said, 'Too right, boss,
Ten bob for a day's a good lurk.'
So he drove the dozen back to his farm
And put them all to work.

Later in the morning,
The farmer returned to the town.
And there in front of the pub he saw
More blokes just sitting down.

'Would you fellas like some work,'
He asked, 'on my farm today?'
He said he'd give them lunch as well
As what was fair in pay.

Each time that farmer went to town,
At nine and twelve and three,
He saw a bunch of unemployed
And said: 'Come and work for me.'

He hired a final bunch of blokes
As late as five—it's true!
Well, when it come to baling hay
There's a lot of work to do.

And then the work was over,
And pay time came around.
The workers then all queued up
Upon the dusty ground.

The ones who were the last to come
Were at the head of the queue.
The farmer said to each one:
'Here's your pay—ten bob for you.'

The ones who'd worked there all the day
Began to make a fuss:
'If these ones each get ten bob,
There'd better be more for us.'

But when the farmer paid them,
They each received the same.
Ten shillings paid to each man,
No matter when he came.

The early ones were boiling mad!
Their union representative
Said: 'This is simply so unfair,
You're being so insensitive.'

The farmer said to the union rep,
'Now listen here, my friend,
I can be generous if I want,
It's my money in the end.

'I've paid your blokes just what I said,
Ten shillings—I kept my word.
If I choose to be kind to others,
No reason for them to be hurt.'

That's how surprising generosity
Turns all our thoughts around.
Astonishing generosity
Turns the whole world upside down.